LITURGIES FOR LITTLE ONES

**38 Celebrations
for
Grades One to Three**

CAROL REZY

All the illustrations in this book
are original creations of the author,
Carol Rezy, and have been redrawn
for publication by Janet Trzaska

**AVE MARIA PRESS
Notre Dame, Indiana 46556**

Nihil Obstat:

    John Allyn Melloh, S.M.
    Censor Deputatus

Imprimatur:

    William E. McManus, D.D.
    Bishop of Fort Wayne-South Bend

Library of Congress Catalog Card Number: 78-59926
International Standard Book Number: 0-87793-160-7

Cover design: Janet Trzaska
Printed and bound in the United States of America.

TABLE OF CONTENTS

INTRODUCTION

How precious you are! You, the teacher of the little ones! Jesus knew how important little children were. He said, "Let the little children come to me, for it is to such as these that the kingdom of heaven belongs" (Mt 19:14-15). How essential your role is as a leader guiding these children to Jesus!

Liturgies for Little Ones is designed to aid you, the teacher, in preparing the children for weekly celebrations of the Eucharist. At the same time they are also an instruction in the life and teachings of Jesus. The book focuses on meaningful themes, simplified liturgies of the word, and the preparation of gifts and hearts for the eucharistic celebration. (Specific petitions, which children can more easily relate to, are indicated in the text and are suggested for use with more general intercessions.)

This book is divided into the nine and one-half months of the school year, and each month—except June—consists of four liturgies. This assumes you have one liturgy per week. Liturgies for special days, such as Halloween, Thanksgiving, Christmas, Valentine's Day, St. Patrick's Day, Mother's Day and Father's Day are also included.

September covers the theme "Me"—which is so important to small children. Throughout the four liturgies, the children become aware of God's unique love for them, and their own distinctiveness.

In October the concept of "Me" is enlarged to include "My Family." This idea will develop even more when God's Family is developed.

November, January and May deal specifically with the teachings of Jesus. Jesus wants us to do many things—to be kind, to be sharing, loving and forgiving, to be peacemakers. He wants us to spread the good news. Each of these topics is dealt with individually in a liturgy.

December is devoted to Advent themes, culminating in a Christmas celebration.

After we have learned about Jesus and some of his teachings, we can begin to follow him. February develops this idea. The children are sure to love the liturgies on fishing, giving and following with footprints.

March and April are concerned with Lent and conclude with an Easter celebration. The last month of the school year, June, contains only two liturgies because it is usually a short school month.

In presenting the theme of the day's liturgy in the classroom, the main idea is explained and discussed with the children in a large group. Following this, small groups are formed. One group designs the banner, another selects appropriate songs and the remainder make offertory gifts, if necessary.

The banner may be made on posterboard or on cardboard having one side white. For special days felt could be used, if your budget allows. The teacher can make the letters or give the children patterns to trace. The rest is up to them. They can discuss what should be put on the banner and how it should be done. You'll be amazed at their creative ideas! We save all our banners and at the end of the school year raffle them off for the children to take home.

Regarding the songs suggested for use in this book, the following five sources were used:

Hi, God! Album and Songbook
Hi, God! 2 Album and Songbook
Come Out Album and Songbook
Songs to Celebrate Life Songbook
Celebrating the Eucharist in Song Songbook

All of these songs were written specifically for children, which accounts for their terrific response. Using guitar instead of organ also adds to the enjoyment. Guidance for the small group selecting the songs will be necessary in the beginning. After a while, however, second- and third-graders should be able to choose songs related to the theme.

I hope you enjoy and have as much fun with **Liturgies for Little Ones** as I have had. Children's liturgies can be made meaningful, for little ones and adults alike. You'll find many parents coming to your liturgies after they have experienced one of them! As for the little ones, they will sing their hearts out . . . become excited in planning . . . will want to do the readings . . . and all will want to design the banners!

Remember, you are the leader . . . the one who guides. As Paul so clearly states in his second letter to the Corinthians: "Thanks be to God who, wherever he goes, makes us, in Christ, partners of his triumph. **Through us,** he is spreading the knowledge of himself, like a sweet smell, everywhere" (II Cor 2:14-15).

THEME:

> We're back together again! Some things we do by ourselves, but many things we do together. We play together. We work together. And today we will pray and sing together. Our friends, moms and dads, and teachers are here to help us celebrate!

READING: I Th 5:23-28 (paraphrased)

> May the God of Peace make you holy. May you always say "Yes" to God. God has called you and will always be with you. Let us pray for each other, brothers and sisters. Welcome everyone with a holy kiss. May Jesus Christ be with you.

RESPONSORIAL PSALM: Pss 133:1,3; 89:15,16; 50:5,6 (paraphrased)

> Refrain: **IT'S GOOD TO BE BACK TOGETHER AGAIN!**

> How good, how delightful it is for all to live together like brothers. God gives us his blessing and his life.

> Happy the people who learn about our God. They will live in his light. They will rejoice in his name all day.

> Let us all be together again before God. Let the heavens praise him.

GOSPEL: Mk 10:13-16 (paraphrased)

> People were bringing little children to him, for him to touch. The disciples turned them away. When Jesus saw this, he said, "Let the little children come to me; do not stop them; for it is to such as these that the Kingdom of God belongs." He put his arms around them, laid his hands on them, and gave them his blessing.

PETITIONS:

Response: **LORD, ANSWER OUR PRAYERS!**

That we can be like Jesus in the way we work this year, we pray to the Lord. . . .

That we will be fair and kind when we play together this year, we pray to the Lord. . . .

That we pray together often, as we are doing today, we pray to the Lord. . . .

PREPARATION OF GIFTS:

Books, paper, pencils, crayons

Ball and bat

Cardboard people

Bread, water and wine

Preparing ourselves:

We first bring up some books, paper, pencils and crayons to show that we work together and help each other.

We also take up a ball and bat. This shows that we will play together this year.

We now take up a chain of people. This chain shows that all of us are back together again!

We offer our love with the bread, water and wine.

SUGGESTED MUSIC:

"Hello Song" by Neil Blunt, **Come Out.**

"Hello, Hello" by Ron Ellis, **Songs to Celebrate Life.**

"Goodbye, Goodbye" by Ron Ellis, **Songs to Celebrate Life.**

BANNER IDEA:

(IN THIS SPACE CHILDREN DRAW PICTURES OF THEMSELVES DOING THINGS TOGETHER)

PATTERN FOR CUT-OUT FIGURES:

Each child makes one "person." Trace the pattern on white construction paper and then cut it out. The children decorate both sides of the cardboard figure as themselves. A mirror may be used to help the children see what they look like. Attach all figures together with yarn securely stapled on the backs.

THEME:

God made each one of us. That makes us special! God is like the potter who forms the clay. He makes each mold special and different. Some of us here are small and some are tall. Some have dark hair, some have light hair. We all look different and feel different things, but God knows each of us very well because he made us. Let's celebrate our own special-ness today!

READING: Eph 1:3-5,11-12 (paraphrased)

Blessed be God our Father who has given us everything. Before the world was made, God chose us to be holy and to live in love. We belong to God. He chose us from the beginning. He chose us to be all that we can be for his greater glory.

RESPONSORIAL PSALM: Ps 139:1-2,13-14,23-24 (paraphrased)

Refrain: **YOU KNOW ME! YOU PUT ME TOGETHER!**

My God, you know me very well. You know if I am standing or sitting. You read my thoughts from far away. You know everything about me.

It was you who created me. You put me together. I thank you for the wonders of myself. I thank you for all your works.

God, you know my heart and my thoughts. Make sure I always follow your way. Always be there to guide me.

GOSPEL: Jn 10:14-15

I am the Good Shepherd. I know my own and my own know me, just as the Father knows me and I know the Father.

PETITIONS:

> Response: **LORD, HEAR OUR PRAYER**
>
> **That we always remember to thank God for all our gifts, we pray to the Lord. . . .**
>
> **That we always remember to thank God for our "special-ness," we pray to the Lord. . . .**
>
> **For all people in the world, so they will see how special they are to us and to God, we pray to the Lord. . . .**

PREPARATION OF GIFTS:

> Big ball of clay.
>
> Three or four items made from clay.
>
> Bread, water and wine.
>
> Preparing ourselves:
>
> **For our offertory gifts, we take up a ball of clay to show that God made us. He is like the potter who molds the clay.**
>
> **We also take up some things made of clay. Each one is different. That's like us! We are all different and very special to God.**
>
> **We now take up the bread, water and wine. They are very special because they will be changed into Jesus very soon.**

SUGGESTED MUSIC:

> "Giant Love Ball Song," **Hi, God!**
>
> "God Made Us All," **Come Out.**
>
> "A Great Beginning," **Songs to Celebrate Life.**
>
> "God Knows Me," **Songs to Celebrate Life.**
>
> "If I Were a Butterfly," **Hi, God! 2.**
>
> "Every Person Is Gift" **Hi, God! 2.**

GIFT IDEA:

Make "I Am Special" ribbons from ribbons or construction paper. Each child wears one of these ribbons during the liturgy and throughout the day.

To extend this idea, pick a "Special Person" every day throughout the school year. Each child gets a turn and also "special privileges," such as being first in line, etc.

BANNER IDEA:

A rainbow is a perfect idea for the banner on being special! All the parts are different colors . . . that's what makes it so beautiful and special!

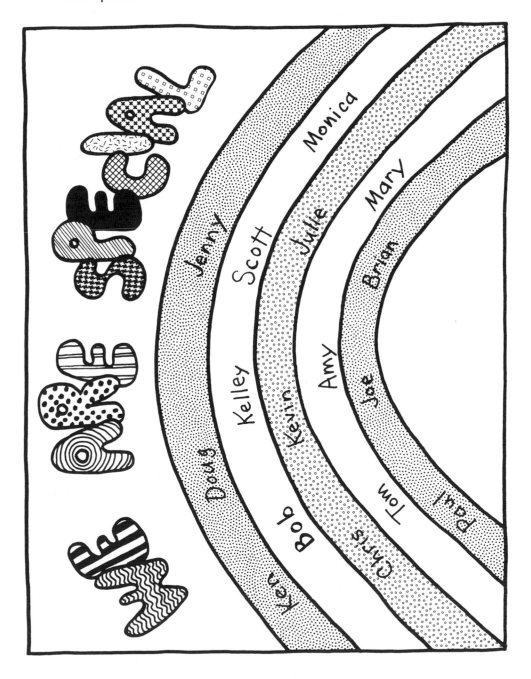

THEME:

> God made all of us! He made each of us different and gave us many things. One of these things is talents. Talents are the things that we can do well. Let's find out what these talents are. Let's use our talents today and every day!

READING: I Cor 12:4-11 (paraphrased)

> There are a lot of gifts, but always the same Spirit. There are a lot of jobs to be done, but we always do them for the same Lord. God is in all people even though he works in different ways. Some people preach, some work miracles. All these gifts are from the same Spirit.

RESPONSORIAL PSALM: Ps 104:1,24,33,34 (paraphrased)

> Refrain: **ALL OUR GIFTS COME FROM GOD!**
>
> Bless Yahweh! He is my God! How great he is! Let us give him glory.
>
> What variety you have created! You have made everything so wisely. The whole earth is full of things you have made!
>
> All creatures depend on you. I will sing to God all my life. I will play for him as long as I live.

GOSPEL: Lk 8:16-18

>No one lights a lamp to cover it with a bowl or to put it under a bed. No, he puts it on a lampstand so that people may see the light when they come in. So take care how you hear; for anyone who has will be given more; from anyone who has not, even what he thinks he has will be taken away.

PETITIONS:

Response: **LORD, HELP US TO USE OUR TALENTS!**

That all of us here may find out what our talents are and use them, we pray to the Lord. . . .

That we may use our talents to show people what Jesus is like, we pray to the Lord. . . .

Let us now add our own intentions in a moment of silence.

PREPARATION OF GIFTS:

Baseball and football
Paper, books and pencils
Two cardboard "persons"
Bread, water and wine

Preparing ourselves:

For our offertory gifts, we take up a baseball and football to show that some of us have talents in sports and games.

We take up paper, books and pencils to show that we try to do our best in our schoolwork.

We also take up two cardboard people to show that all of us try to use our talents to be good friends.

We now take up the bread, water and wine. Jesus gave us himself.

SUGGESTED MUSIC:

"God Made Us All," **Come Out.**
"All Your Gifts of Life," **Hi, God! 2.**
"Giant Love Ball Song," **Hi, God!**

BANNER IDEA:

Turn your banner into a big crossword puzzle! Use these words or any words you and the children have discussed with regard to talents.

THEME:

God has given us many things! One very special gift we have is our friends. It's good, so good to have friends. We can play with them. We can talk to them. And our friends are always around to help us. How lucky we are to have friends!

READING: Sir 6:14-17 (paraphrased)

A faithful friend is a sure shelter. Whoever finds one has found a real treasure. A faithful friend is something beyond price. You cannot measure his worth. Those who love the Lord will find real friends.

RESPONSORIAL PSALM: Prov 16:7; 17:17; 18:19 (paraphrased)

Refrain: **FRIENDS ALWAYS SHOW THEIR LOVE!**

When you please the Lord by the way you live, you can make your enemies into friends.

Friends also show their love. What are brothers for, if not to share their troubles?

Brothers helping each other is a fortress. Friends are like the bars of a strong castle.

GOSPEL: Jn 15:12-15 (paraphrased)

This is my commandment: love one another as I have loved you and you will be happy. You are my friends if you do what I tell you. I will not call you servants anymore. A servant does not know his master's business. I call you friends because I have told you everything that I have learned from my Father.

PETITIONS:

Response: **HELP US TO BE REAL FRIENDS.**

That we may love and be kind to our friends, we pray to the Lord. . . .

For all the lonely people who need friends, let us pray to the Lord. . . .

That we may see you, Jesus, in all the people we meet, we pray to the Lord. . . .

PREPARATION OF GIFTS:

Large "Garden of Friends" banner to put on altar

Straw basket of construction-paper flowers
   (children make flowers, each with his or her own name and
   the name of a friend)

Bread, water and wine

Preparing ourselves:

For our gifts to God, we take up a banner to show that God gives us many, many friends.

We also take up a basket of paper flowers. These flowers are for our friends who are so special to us.

We now take up the bread, water and wine to show that Jesus is our friend, too. He wants us to be his friends, too.

SUGGESTED MUSIC:

"To Be a Friend," **Come Out.**

"Ray, the Rangy Rhino," **Come Out.**

"Friends, Friends, Friends," **Hi, God! 2.**

"Friends Are Like Flowers," **Hi, God! 2.**

Use a straw basket with a handle for the offertory gift. Make flowers from construction paper. The children can decorate the flowers and put their own names and that of a friend on. Make the basket overflowing!

BANNER IDEA:

Make a large banner for the offertory procession. It will be hung on the front of the altar. Children can decorate it with the sun, clouds, flowers, birds, etc. Have the children write their names on the objects in the banner.

THEME:

> We all belong to a family! We have moms and dads and some of us have brothers and sisters. Some families are small and some are big. Let's celebrate and thank God today for giving us our families.

READING: Eph 3:14-19 (paraphrased)

> Every family, whether spiritual or natural, takes its name from God our Father. From his love, he has given us the power to grow strong, so that Christ will live in our hearts and, knowing God's love, we will be full.

RESPONSORIAL PSALM: Sir 7:27-28; 3:2,6 (paraphrased)

> Refrain: **YOU WILL HAVE LONG LIFE IF YOU OBEY YOUR MOTHER AND FATHER!**

> Honor your father and mother with all your heart. How can you repay them for all they have done for you?

> The Lord honors the father of his children. He upholds the rights of a mother over her children.

> You will have long life if you honor your father. You will be obeying God if you honor your mother.

GOSPEL: Jn 17:23 (paraphrased)

> With me in them and you in me, may they be so completely one that the world will realize that it was you who sent me. I have loved them as much as you loved me.

PETITIONS:

Response: **LORD, BLESS OUR FAMILIES!**

For our moms and dads who love us very much and always take care of us and help us, we pray to the Lord. . . .

For our brothers and sisters . . . bless them, Jesus, and make them happy, we pray to the Lord. . . .

For all families in the world, so they will be filled with love and happiness, we pray to the Lord. . . .

PREPARATION OF GIFTS:

Picture of a family
Cardboard people—mother, father, brother, sister
Bread, water and wine

Preparing ourselves:

We take up a picture of a family. We love our families and like to do things with them.

We also take up a family of people. On the figures we have drawn pictures and written the names of the people in our families.

We now take up the bread, water and wine. God our Father gave us his Son, Jesus, so we could be strong and one with him.

SUGGESTED MUSIC:

"Belonging," **Celebrating the Eucharist in Song.**
"Song for Everyone," **Songs to Celebrate Life.**
"Thank You, Lord," **Hi, God!**

GIFT IDEA:

Make four cardboard people of different sizes. They will represent
the mother, father, brother and sister in families. The children write
their brothers', sisters', mom's and dad's names on the figures. They
can bring in pictures or draw pictures on the figures.

BANNER IDEA:

THEME:

Each of us has a family with a mom and dad, brothers and sisters. But
we also belong to a bigger family—the biggest family of all! That's
God's family! We become part of his family by being baptized.
Let's celebrate belonging to God's family today!

READING: Tit 3:4-7 (paraphrased)

Our kind and loving God has saved us. He has saved us by living
water and has given us a new beginning. He has put the Holy Spirit
in us and we have become part of the family of God. We will share
in his life and hope forever.

RESPONSORIAL PSALM: Is 63:8,16; 64:7-8 (paraphrased)

Refrain: **WE BELONG TO THE FAMILY OF GOD!**

He said, "Truly they are my people, they are my sons."

You, Yahweh, you yourself are our Father; "Our Redeemer" is your
name.

Yahweh, you are our Father. We are the clay, you the potter. We
are all the work of your hand.

GOSPEL: Jn 3:5,7,8 (paraphrased)

I tell you, unless a man is born through water and the Spirit, he
cannot enter the kingdom of God. Do not be surprised at what I say:
You must be born from above. That is how it is with all who are born
of the Spirit.

PETITIONS:

Response: **LORD, FILL US WITH YOUR LOVE!**

For all the people in the world who belong to the family of God, we pray to the Lord. . . .

For all people, so they will come to love you as much as we do, we pray to the Lord. . . .

So we can help one another to act as good children of God, we pray to the Lord. . . .

PREPARATION OF GIFTS:

Picture of a family
Globe
Bread, water and wine

Preparing ourselves:

For our gifts to God, we take up a picture of a family to show that each one of us belongs to a family at home.

We also take up a globe. Baptized people all over the world belong to God's family.

We offer ourselves and all our love with the bread, water and wine.

SUGGESTED MUSIC:

"Belonging," **Celebrating the Eucharist in Song.**
"Songs for Everyone" **Songs to Celebrate Life.**
"Song of Baptism," **Hi, God!**

BANNER IDEA:

Children draw a picture of the world showing that God's family is all over the world.

THEME:

We are part of God's House! Many houses are made of nails, wood and bricks, but God builds his house with people. People like you and like me!

READING: Eph 2:19-22 (paraphrased)

You are no longer visitors. You are like the saints; you are part of God's House. You are part of a building that has the apostles and prophets for its foundations. Jesus Christ is the cornerstone. You are being built into a house where God lives. You are growing in the Spirit.

RESPONSORIAL PSALM: Ps 122:1,8,9 (paraphrased)

Refrain: **LET US GO TO THE HOUSE OF THE LORD!**

I was so happy when they said to me, "Let us go to the house of God!"

Since all my brothers and friends are here, I say "Peace be with you!"

Since our God lives here, I pray that you will be happy.

GOSPEL: Mt 7:24-27 (paraphrased)

Everyone who listens to my words and acts on them will be like a sensible man who built his house on rock. Rain came down, floods rose, gales blew against that house, and it did not fall. It was founded on rock. But everyone who listens to my words and does not act on them will be like a silly man who built his house on sand. Rain came down, floods rose, gales blew against that house, and it fell. And what a fall it had!

PETITIONS:

Response: **LORD, HELP US TO BE GOOD MEMBERS OF YOUR HOUSE!**

So all of us here today will try to be good followers of Jesus, we pray to the Lord. . . .

For all the people in the world who are without homes, we pray to the Lord. . . .

Dear Jesus, help us to remember we are part of your house and you are the head of this house, we pray to the Lord. . . .

PREPARATION OF GIFTS:

Doll house
Bricks, nails and wood
Collage containing the children's pictures
Bread, water and wine

Preparing ourselves:

For our gifts to God, we take up a house to show that there are many different kinds of houses.

We also take up some bricks, nails and wood to show that people build their houses from these things.

But God builds his house with people! We now bring up a picture of all of us! We all are part of God's house!

We bring up the bread, water and wine. They will be changed into Jesus, who is the head of this house.

SUGGESTED MUSIC:

"God Is Building a House," **Hi, God! 2.**
"Great Things Happen," **Hi, God!**
"We Are the Body of Christ," **Hi, God! 2.**
"Come and Go With Me" **Hi, God! 2.**

BANNER IDEA:

Make your banner into a big house. . . .

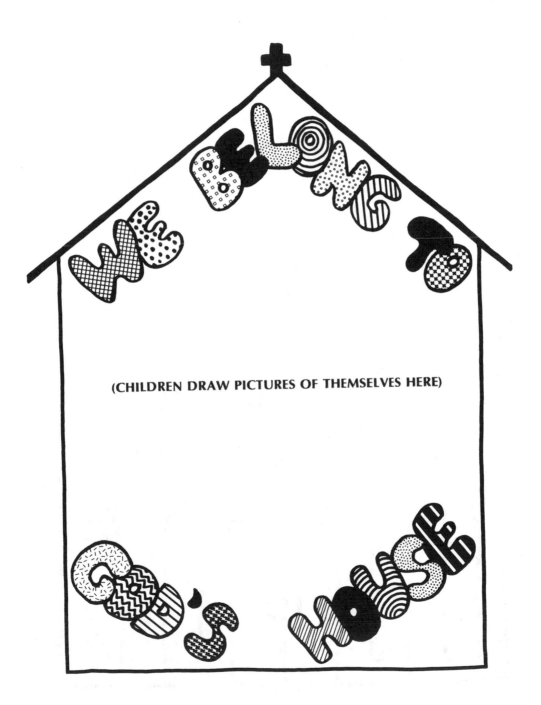

(CHILDREN DRAW PICTURES OF THEMSELVES HERE)

AT THE SIGN OF PEACE . . .
Have the children make little houses like the one below.
Make the houses of brightly colored construction paper—
reds, blues, yellows, oranges, greens, etc. At the Sign of Peace, the
children exchange the houses and say "Peace be with you! You
belong to God's House!"

As background music during the Sign of Peace, "God Is Building a
House" from the album **Hi God! 2** could be played.

THEME:

> Halloween is a time to dress up and to wear masks. No one knows who we are when we wear our costumes! But Halloween lasts only one day and then we take off our masks. We become ourselves again . . . the special person God made us to be. How good it is to be ourselves again!

READING: Gen 27:1-34 (paraphrased)

> Isaac called his son, Esau. He said to him, "My son, I am old and my eyes are weak. I do not know when I may die. Go into the country and hunt me some game. Make the meal I like so I can eat it. Then I will give you my blessing before I die." Isaac's wife, Rebekah, heard them talking. She told their other son, Jacob, about this. She told him to go hunt the game and bring it back so she could cook the meal for Isaac. Then Jacob would receive the blessing. But Jacob said, "My brother is a hairy man, but I am smooth-skinned. I will be cursed, instead of blessed, if I try to trick my father." But his mother said it was all right. She covered Jacob's arms with goats' skin so they would be hairy and gave the meal to Isaac. Isaac thought it was his son Esau and gave him the blessing. But Isaac had been tricked.

RESPONSORIAL PSALM: Jer 1:5; Is 43:1,7 (paraphrased)

> Refrain: **I HAVE FORMED YOU AND MADE YOU!**
>
> **Before I formed you, I knew you. Before you were ever born, I made you holy.**
>
> **You are precious in my eyes. You are honored and I love you.**
>
> **You have my name; I created you for my glory. I have formed you and made you.**

GOSPEL: Lk 12:1-2 (paraphrased)

Meanwhile the crowds of people gathered around Jesus. He first spoke to his apostles: "Be on your guard against the yeast of the Pharisees—that is, their hypocrisy. Everything that is now covered will be uncovered, and everything now hidden will be made clear."

PETITIONS:

Response: **LORD, HELP US TO BE OURSELVES!**

That we can take off our masks and be ourselves, we pray to the Lord. . . .

That all people come to know who they really are, we pray to the Lord. . . .

That we remember to thank you for making us, we pray to the Lord. . . .

PREPARATION OF GIFTS:

Halloween masks
Mirror
Bread, water and wine

Preparing ourselves:

For our gifts, we take up some of our Halloween masks. These show that we sometimes wear masks and pretend to be someone else.

We also take up a mirror. When we look in a mirror, we see ourselves as we really are . . . that special person God made.

We now take up the bread, water and wine with our love.

SUGGESTED MUSIC:

"Halloween Song," **Come Out.**
"God Made Us All," **Come Out.**
"A Great Beginning," **Songs to Celebrate Life.**

BANNER IDEA:

Make a BIG Halloween ghost for your banner! At Halloween we put on masks and pretend to be someone else. After the special day, let's remember to be ourselves again!

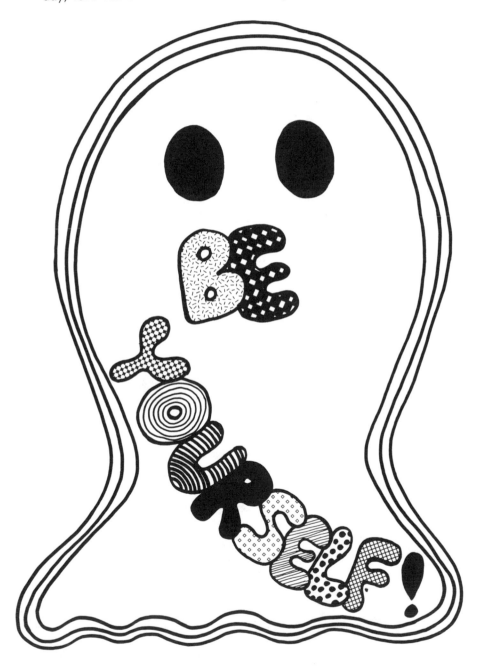

THEME:

> One of the things Jesus teaches us is how to share! Jesus always shared his time with people. He talked with them and healed them. He also shared his love and talents. Let's try to be like Jesus in the way we share!

READING: Job 31:16-20,37 (paraphrased)

> I have not been insensible to a poor man's needs. I have taken bread for myself and shared it with an orphan. I have shared my clothes with a beggar so he could be warm. God knows my life and the way I live.

RESPONSORIAL PSALM: Prov 3:27; 11:25; 19;6 (paraphrased)

> Refrain: **A MAN WHO SHARES MAKES LOTS OF FRIENDS!**

> Do not refuse a kindness to anyone who begs. It is in your power to share.

> The generous, sharing person will be happy. He who shares will be prosperous.

> The man who shares makes lots of friends.

GOSPEL: Lk 11:37-42 (paraphrased)

> Jesus had just finished speaking when a Pharisee invited him to dinner. He went in and sat down at the table. The Pharisee saw that he did not wash before the meal. But Jesus said to him, "Oh, you Pharisees! You clean the outside of a cup and plate, while inside yourselves you are filled with wickedness. Fools! Did not he who made the outside also make the inside? Instead, share what you have and then everything will be clean for you."

PETITIONS:

>Response: **HELP US TO SHARE AS YOU DID, JESUS!**
>
>**For all of us, so we can share our things with others, we pray to the Lord. . . .**
>
>**For people who do not like to share, we pray to the Lord. . . .**
>
>**That we remember to share our talents, to make others happy. . . .**

PREPARATION OF GIFTS:

>Three or four toys
>Clock
>Big paper heart
>Poster (with words and pictures of some of our talents)
>Bread, water and wine

>Preparing ourselves:
>
>**We take some of our toys to remind us to share our games and the things we have with others.**
>
>**We also take up a clock. This reminds us to share our time when others need us.**
>
>**We take up a heart to show how we want to share our love with other people.**
>
>**We now take up a poster of our talents. God gave us many things that we can do well; these are talents. He gave them to us to share.**
>
>**We take up the bread, water and wine. God gave us his Son, Jesus, so we can learn how to live.**

SUGGESTED MUSIC:

>"It's Up To Us," **Come Out.**
>"She's Just an Old Stump!" **Come Out.**
>"What God Is Like," **Hi, God! 2.**
>"Love That Is Kept Inside," **Hi, God!**
>"Reach Out!" **Hi, God!**

BANNER IDEA:

For I was hungry and you gave me food, I was thirsty and you gave me drink. I was a stranger and you welcomed me, naked and you clothed me. I was ill and you comforted me, in pris... visi...

KINDNESS

THEME:

Jesus was always very kind to the people he met. He talked with the people, healed them and helped them. Jesus wants us to be kind, too! Not just to our families and friends, but to all the people we meet!

READING: Col 3:12,14,15 (paraphrased)

You are God's chosen race, his saints, and he loves you. You should be forgiving, kind, gentle and patient. Be all of these things and be loving. May the peace of Christ be in your hearts.

RESPONSORIAL PSALM: Ps 107:8-9,43; 112:9 (paraphrased)

Refrain: **BE QUICK TO BE GENEROUS AND GIVE TO THE POOR!**

Let us thank Yahweh for his love and for all the marvelous things he has done for us.

Quick to be generous, he gives to the poor. If a man acts like this, he will be honored.

If you are wise, you will study these things and realize how Yahweh shows us his love.

GOSPEL: Mt 25:34-36,40 (paraphrased)

Come, you whom my Father has blessed, take the kingdom that has been prepared for you. For I was hungry, and you gave me food; I was thirsty, and you gave me drink; I was a stranger and you made me welcome; naked and you clothed me; sick and you visited me; in prison and you came to see me. I tell you, insofar as you do this to one of my brothers, you do it to me.

PETITIONS:

Response: **HELP US TO BE KIND LIKE YOU WERE, JESUS!**

That we remember to help the people who need us, we pray to the Lord. . . .

For all our unhappy, sick and hungry brothers and sisters in the world, we pray to the Lord. . . .

For all the forgotten people, we pray to the Lord. . . .

PREPARATION OF GIFTS:

Basket of hearts
Chain of hearts
Bread, water and wine

Preparing ourselves:

We take up a basket of hearts. We have put our names on the hearts to show that all of us are trying to be kind like Jesus.

We also take up a chain of hearts as a gift to God. On each heart are written ways in which we can be kind to the people we know and the people we meet.

We offer ourselves and all our kind acts with the bread, water and wine.

SUGGESTED MUSIC:

"Let's Go Forth," **Celebrating the Eucharist in Song.**
"Caring," **Celebrating the Eucharist in Song.**
"People Who Care," **Songs to Celebrate Life.**
"Happiness," **Songs to Celebrate Life.**
"This Is My Commandment," **Hi, God! 2.**
"Our God Is a God of Love," **Hi, God! 2.**

GIFT IDEA:

The pattern for the hearts is below. Have each child make a heart. Have each child write his name on the heart and decorate it. Collect all the hearts and put them in a wicker basket to carry up and set on the altar at offertory time. We are all trying to be kind like Jesus!

Use the same size heart for the paper chain. On each of the hearts, the children write ways in which they can be kind to someone. Staple yarn to the hearts and hang from the altar.

At the Sign of Peace, the children could exchange hearts. On the hearts could be a kind saying for that person.

PRAYING TO GOD

Please knock

THEME:

When you love someone, you like to be with him and talk to him. That's what praying is all about! Praying is being with God and listening and talking to him. Let's show God how much we love him by praying to him in a special way today at Mass!

READING: Eph 6:18 (paraphrased)

Pray all the time, asking for what you need, praying in the Spirit every day. Never get tired of staying awake to pray for all the saints. I pray that I can spread the gospel like I should.

RESPONSORIAL PSALM: Pss 61:1-2; 88:1-2; 116:1-2 (paraphrased)

Refrain: **GOD LISTENS WHEN WE CALL!**

God, hear my cry for help; listen to my prayer! I call to you with all my heart.

I call for help all day and all night. May my prayer reach you.

I am happy! God listens to my prayers. He bends down to listen to me when I call.

GOSPEL: Mt 7:7-11

Ask, and it will be given to you; search and you will find; knock, and the door will be opened to you. For the one who asks always receives; the one who searches always finds; the one who knocks will always have the door opened to him. Is there a man among you who would hand his son a stone when he asked for bread? Or would hand him a snake when he asked for a fish? If you, then, who are evil, know how to give your children what is good, how much more will your Father in heaven give good things to those who ask him!

PETITIONS:

> Response: **LORD, LISTEN TO OUR PRAYERS!**
>
> **For our families and friends, that their prayers will be answered. We pray to the Lord. . . .**
>
> **For all the sick and unhappy people, we pray to the Lord. . . .**
>
> **For those people who forget to pray to you, we pray to the Lord. . . .**

PREPARATION OF GIFTS:

> Prayer chain
> Cardboard door with words "Knock and the door will be opened to you"
> Bread, water and wine
>
> Preparing ourselves:
>
> **We first take up a prayer chain for our offertory gifts. On this chain we have written prayers to God.**
>
> **We also take up a door. Jesus told us "knock and the door will be opened to you." Jesus tells us he will answer our prayers if we ask him.**
>
> **We now offer our love to God with the bread, water and wine.**

SUGGESTED MUSIC:

> "Celebrating," **Celebrating the Eucharist in Song.**
> "Listen," **Celebrating the Eucharist in Song.**
> "Show and Tell," **Songs to Celebrate Life.**
> "Celebrate God," **Hi, God!**
> "I Believe in the Sun," **Hi, God!**
> "Listen, Listen," **Hi, God!**

BANNER IDEA:

GIFT IDEAS:

Use brightly colored construction paper. The children compose and write their prayers on one strip of paper. Staple the strips together to make a chain. Hang it around and on the altar as a decoration.

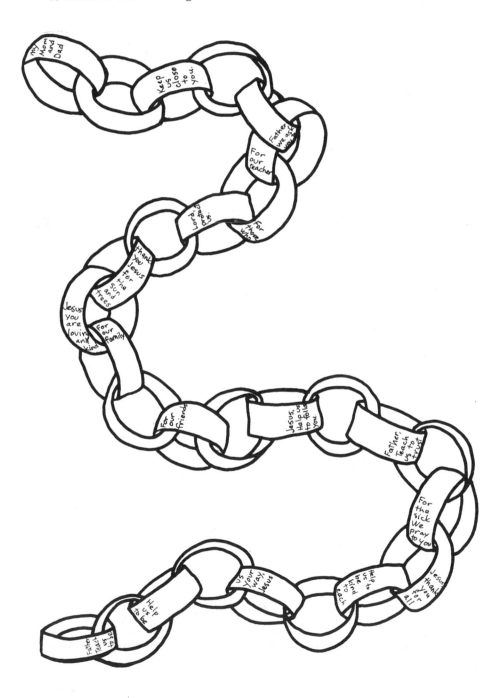

Make a cardboard door with the words "Knock and the door will be opened to you." Make the door big, the bigger the better!

THEME:

Today is a special day! It is Thanksgiving! It's the day we thank God for all the things he has given us. Think of all the things we can be thankful for: our families and friends, our food and clothes, our school and teachers, and all the love in the world. Let's celebrate our thanks to God today!

READING: Sir 39:14-15,35 (paraphrased)

Sing a song of praise to bless the Lord for all his works! Tell him how great he is! Give him praise with song and with lyre. Sing with all your heart and voice. Bless the name of the Lord for all his works!

RESPONSORIAL PSALM: Ps 136:1,4-6,7-9,25-26 (paraphrased)

Refrain: **GIVE THANKS TO THE LORD, FOR HE IS GOOD!**

Give thanks to the Lord for he is good. He made the heavens, the earth, and the waters.

He performs great things. He made the great lights—the sun, the moon and the stars.

He gives us all we need. He loves us forever! Give thanks to our God! He loves us forever!

GOSPEL: Lk 17:11-17 (paraphrased)

On his way to Jerusalem, Jesus entered one of the villages. He met 10 lepers. They called to him, "Jesus! Master! Take pity on us!" He said to them, "Go and show yourselves to the priests." As they went away, they were cured. One of them came back and praised God at the top of his voice. He knelt in front of Jesus and thanked him. This made Jesus say, "Were not all 10 made clean? Where are the other nine? It seems that no one has come back to give praise to God, except this one."

PETITIONS:

Response: **LORD, HEAR OUR PRAYER!**

That we always remember to thank God for all the things he has given us, we pray to the Lord. . . .

For all the people in the world who do not have the gifts that we share here today, we pray to the Lord. . . .

For all the sick, poor and lonely people. Fill them with your love and happiness on this Thanksgiving Day, we pray to the Lord. . . .

PREPARATION OF GIFTS:

Picture of family
Basket of food and clothes
"THANKS" sign
Bread, water and wine

Preparing ourselves:

We take up a picture of a family. God gives us our family and friends to love.

We also take up a basket of food and some clothes. God always takes care of us. He gives us the things we need.

To show that we are thankful for all God's gifts, we take up a big "THANK YOU" sign to put on the altar.

We also take up the bread, water and wine. God also gave us the best gift of all—Jesus in Communion.

SUGGESTED MUSIC:

"All Your Gifts of Life," **Hi, God! 2.**
"Thank You, Lord," **Hi, God!**
"Thank You, Lord," **Songs to Celebrate Life.**

GIFT IDEA:

Draw the word THANKS on two sheets of white paper. Make sure the letters overlap so it will stand freely. Cut out the word and glue it to some cardboard with the same shape as the word. Have the children color the letters. When put on the altar, it can be leaned against the microphone, or a piece of cardboard could be attached to the back of the sign to help it stand.

BANNER IDEA:

THANKSGIVING:

(IN THIS SPACE CHILDREN DRAW PICTURES OF THINGS FOR WHICH THEY ARE THANKFUL)

A TIME TO GIVE THANKS

THEME:

Everyone thought John the Baptist was a strange man! He lived in the desert, wore camel hair, and ate locusts. But John was very special! He told the people to stop saying "No" to God and to get ready for Jesus. He prepared the way for the Lord. We, too, should get ready on the inside! What are you doing to get ready when Jesus comes at Christmas?

READING: Eph 4:22-24 (paraphrased)

You must give up your old way of life. You must put away your old self. You must renew your mind and put on a new self. The new self will be created in God's way. It will be good and holy.

RESPONSORIAL PSALM: Ps 37:3,23,27 (paraphrased)

Refrain: **LET US PUT ON A NEW SELF!**

Trust in God and do what is good. Make your home in the land and live in peace. Make God your only joy.

God guides our steps. He is happy when we do good. We may fall, but God is always there to help us.

Never do what is wrong. Always try to do good. God loves what is right and he is here to help us.

GOSPEL: Mk 1:1-8 (paraphrased)

And so John the Baptist appeared in the wilderness. John wore a garment of camel skin, and he lived on locusts and wild honey. He said: "Prepare a way for the Lord; make his paths straight." All the people came to him and were baptized by him. While Jesus was preaching, John told the people, "Someone is following me, who is more powerful than I. I baptize you with water, but he will baptize you with the Holy Spirit."

58

PETITIONS:

Response: **JESUS, HELP US TO GET READY!**

So we can put away the bad things we do and start doing good deeds, we pray to the Lord. . . .

So we can try to be more helpful to our parents, teachers and friends, we pray to the Lord. . . .

So we can show Jesus how much we love him by the things we say and the things we do, we pray to the Lord. . . .

PREPARATION OF GIFTS:

Cross
Sandals and sheepskin
Bread, water and wine

Preparing ourselves:

For our gifts to God, we take up a cross to show that God forgives us for the times we say "No" to him.

We also take up a pair of sandals and a sheepskin to stand for John the Baptist. John told the people to stop saying "No" to God and to start saying "Yes" and to get ready for Jesus to come.

We offer our love and good deeds with the bread, water and wine.

SUGGESTED MUSIC:

"Come, Lord Jesus," **Hi, God! 2.**
"Happiness," **Songs to Celebrate Life.**
"It's Up to Us," **Come Out.**

BANNER IDEA:

START SAYING

(IN THIS SPACE CHILDREN DRAW PICTURES OF THAT
"STRANGE MAN—JOHN THE BAPTIST"
BY THE RIVER, WITH JESUS, ETC.)

YES!

THEME:

(Children process in, carrying things that give off light: candles, flashlights, light bulbs, etc.)

Jesus says "I am the Light of the World." Street lights, flashlights, and candles are some things that give us light. We, too, have a light inside us! Jesus wants us to let our light shine! Let your light shine by the good things you do!

READING: 1 John 1:5-7 (paraphrased)

This is the message I give you: God is light. There is no darkness in him at all. If we live in light, as he is our light, we are in union together. Let us walk together in the light.

RESPONSORIAL PSALM: Ps 27:1, Is 9:1; 60:19 (paraphrased)

Refrain: **GOD IS MY LIGHT!**

God is my light and my salvation. He is my fortress. Whom should I fear?

The people who walked in darkness have seen a light. A light has shone for those who live in a deep shadow.

God is my everlasting light. He is my splendor and happiness.

GOSPEL: Jn 7:12

When Jesus spoke to the people again, he said: "I am the light of the world. Anyone who follows me will not be walking in the dark; he will have the light of life."

PETITIONS:

Response: **HELP US TO WALK IN YOUR LIGHT!**

May we let our light shine by helping others who need us. For this we pray to the Lord. . . .

So we can become more and more like Jesus every day, we pray to the Lord. . . .

So we can let our light shine by praying for people who need your help, we pray to the Lord. . . .

PREPARATION OF GIFTS:

Light bulb
Flashlight
Candle
Picture of Jesus
Bread, water and wine

Preparing ourselves:

For our Offertory gifts, we take up a light bulb, flashlight and a candle to show that these things give us light in our world. They help us to see.

We now take up a picture of Jesus. Jesus is our light. He lights up the path to God our Father. He helps us to see the right way to live.

We take up the bread, water and wine. They will be changed into Jesus, the light of the world.

SUGGESTED MUSIC:

"Children of the Lord," **Hi, God! 2.**
"Children of Light," **Come Out.**
"I've Got a Light," **Songs to Celebrate Life.**

BANNER IDEA:

Put the children's names inside the light bulb. Each of us has a light inside . . . let it shine!!

THEME:

> The Jesse Tree is like a family tree! The decorations hung on the tree show us all the people who waited for Jesus to come. We are also waiting for Jesus to come! He will be coming soon!

READING: Is 11:10 (paraphrased)

> On the day, the root of Jesse will be a sign to all the people in the world. Everyone will look for it. The Lord will raise his hand once more to save his people and will gather them from the four corners of the earth.

RESPONSORIAL PSALM: Ps 135:1, 5-6, 19-20 (paraphrased)

> Refrain: **PRAISE OUR LORD, FOR HE IS GOOD!**

> Praise our Lord, everyone, for he is good! God rules the heavens, the earth, and the oceans.

> Your name will last forever! You love your people and care for them.

> House of Israel, bless the Lord! House of Aaron, bless the Lord! House of Levi, bless the Lord!

GOSPEL: Mk 1:3

> Look, I am going to send my messenger before you; he will prepare your way. A voice cries in the wilderness: Prepare a way for the Lord, make his paths straight.

PETITIONS:

Response: **COME, LORD JESUS!**

Jesus, while we are waiting for you, help us to show our love to the people around us. We pray to the Lord. . . .

May all people be filled with your happiness and love on Christmas Day. We pray to the Lord. . . .

Dear Jesus, please come soon. We pray to the Lord. . . .

PREPARATION OF GIFTS:

JESSE TREE ORNAMENTS (prior to this, the Jesse Tree should be set up and have some of the ornaments on it. The rest of the ornaments are brought up and explained at the offertory now).

One or two wrapped Christmas presents (empty)

Bread, water and wine

Preparing ourselves:

We take up some of the Jesse Tree ornaments now. Our first ornaments are a picture of Mary and some tools. These show that Mary and Joseph waited for Jesus to come.

Our next ornament is a picture of some water. This stands for John the Baptist. John told the people to get ready for Jesus. He told the people to stop saying "No" to God and to start saying "Yes."

We also bring up some people made of cardboard to put on our Jesse Tree. This shows that we are also waiting for Jesus to come to us on Christmas Day.

We now take up a Christmas present. It is still empty because we are still waiting for Jesus to come.

We now take up the bread, water and wine. We offer our love with these gifts.

SUGGESTED MUSIC:

"The Jesse Tree Song," **Come Out.**

"Come, Lord Jesus," **Hi, God! 2.**

Advent Songs from the hymnal.

PATTERNS FOR JESSE TREE ORNAMENTS:

ADAM AND EVE—PART OF AN APPLE
Genesis 1 and 2

NOAH—ARK WITH A RAINBOW
Genesis 9:12-17

ABRAHAM—ALTAR OF STONE
Genesis 12-22

JOSEPH—COAT OF MANY COLORS
Genesis 37

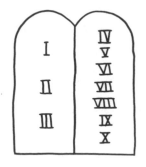

MOSES—THE 10 COMMANDMENTS
Exodus 20:1-17

JONAH—WHALE
Jonah 1 and 2

MARY—CHILD-DRAWN PICTURE OF MARY
Luke 1:26-38

JOSEPH—TOOLS
Matthew 1:18-25

JOHN THE BAPTIST—WATER
Mark 1:1-8

WE WAIT FOR JESUS, TOO!
CARDBOARD PEOPLE

THEME:

Here it is! The day has finally arrived! It is Christmas; the birthday of Jesus! May all of you here have a very Merry Christmas!

READING: Is 9:1-2 (paraphrased)

The people that walked in darkness have seen a great light. On those who live in darkness, a great light has shone. You have given them gladness and joy. They rejoice in you.

RESPONSORIAL PSALM: Is 60:1,4,5 (paraphrased)

Refrain: **RISE, SHINE OUT, FOR YOUR LIGHT HAS COME!**

Rise, shine out, for your light has come. The glory of God is rising on you.

Lift up your eyes and look around. All are gathering and coming to you.

At this sight, you will grow radiant. Your heart will be full and it will throb.

GOSPEL: Lk 2:1-20 (paraphrased)

At this time, Caesar Augustus said that all the people must be counted. The people were to go to their own towns to be counted. So Joseph and Mary, who was with child, set out for the town of Bethlehem. When they were there, Mary gave birth to a son, a baby boy. She wrapped him in swaddling clothes and laid him in a manger. An angel appeared now to some shepherds who were nearby. The shepherds were frightened, but the angel said, "Do not be afraid. I bring good news . . . news of joy. Today a savior has been born to you. He is Christ the Lord." When the angels had gone, the shepherds hurried to Bethlehem and found Mary, Joseph, and the baby lying in the manger. They told Mary and Joseph what the angels said to them. Mary treasured all these things in her heart. And the shepherds went away praising God for all they had seen and heard.

PETITIONS:

Response: **LORD, HEAR OUR PRAYER**

That all people will be happy on this birthday of Jesus, we pray to the Lord. . . .

That there will be love and peace in the world today and every day, we pray to the Lord. . . .

That the joy and peace of Christmas will last every day, we pray to the Lord. . . .

PREPARATION OF GIFTS:

Crib with baby Jesus inside
Birthday card
Candle
Bread, water and wine

Preparing ourselves:

For our gifts on this Christmas Day, we take up a crib carrying Baby Jesus. Jesus has come—for you and me.

We also take up a birthday card for Jesus to celebrate this special day.

We now take up a candle to show that today a great light shines. Today Jesus is born.

We also take up the bread, water and wine . . . our gift to God.

SUGGESTED MUSIC:

"A Violet in the Snow," **Hi, God! 2.**
Christmas Carols.

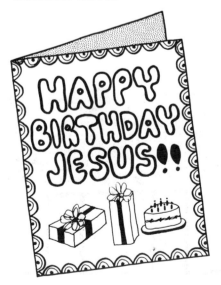

For one of the offertory gifts, take up a birthday card for for Jesus. Let the children make and decorate it. Make it big for all to see. The bigger the better! And all the children can sign their names on the inside. Display it on or near the altar.

BANNER IDEA:

(IN THIS SPACE CHILDREN DRAW PICTURES)

JANUARY

TELL ME ABOUT JESUS

THEME:

> Jesus was kind and forgiving. He said good things about people and he never fought with anyone. This is what a peacemaker is! Jesus wants us to be like him and be peacemakers, too!

READING: Eph 4:25-27, 29-32 (paraphrased)

> So from now on, there must be no more lies: you must speak the truth to one another, since we are parts of one another. Even if you are angry, you must not sin; never let the sun set on your anger. Do not say bad things about one another. Do good to your listeners. Never hold grudges or lose your temper, or raise your voice to anyone, or call one another names. Be friends with one another; be kind, and forgive as readily as God forgives you.

RESPONSORIAL PSALM: Is 26:12; 54:10; 9:6 (paraphrased)

> Refrain: **YAHWEH, YOU GIVE US PEACE!**
>
> Yahweh, you give us peace. You treat us the way we deserve.
>
> Wide is your rule in a peace that will never end.
>
> You will never leave us. Your peace will never be shaken.

GOSPEL: Mt 11:28-30 (paraphrased)

> Come to me, all you who labor and are overburdened, and I will give you peace. Shoulder my yoke and learn from me, for I am gentle and humble of heart, and you will find peace for your souls. Yes, my yoke is easy and my burden light.

PETITIONS:

Response: **JESUS, HELP US TO BE PEACEMAKERS!**

So we can be kind and forgiving, we pray to the Lord. . . .

So we can say only good things about people, we pray to the Lord. . . .

For all people who find it hard to be good peacemakers, we pray to the Lord. . . .

PREPARATION OF GIFTS:

Broken heart (construction paper)
Mended heart (construction paper)
Bread, water and wine

Preparing ourselves:

We take up a broken heart to show what it is like when we are not peacemakers, and instead we hurt someone by words or by something we do.

We now take up a mended heart to show what it is like when we are peacemakers and not hurting . . . when we are kind and forgiving.

We take up the bread, water and wine. They will be changed into Jesus, our Peacemaker.

SUGGESTED MUSIC:

"Making Peace," **Celebrating the Eucharist in Song.**
"Happy the Heart," **Hi, God!**
"Peace Time," **Hi, God!**
"P-E-A-C-E," **Come Out.**
"What Shall I Do?" **Hi, God! 2.**
"Peace Is Flowing Like a River," **Hi, God! 2.**
"Jesus, Jesus," **Hi, God! 2.**

BANNER IDEA:

THEME:

> When Jesus worked miracles, he also forgave the sins of people. Jesus tells us we must forgive one another if we want God to forgive us. Let's remember these words of Jesus.

READING: Col 3:12-13 (paraphrased)

> You are God's chosen race, his saints. He loves you. Bear with one another. Forgive each other as soon as a quarrel begins. The Lord has forgiven you; now you must do the same.

RESPONSORIAL PSALM: Pss 32:1,5; 103:2-3 (paraphrased)

> Refrain: **YOU HAVE FORGIVEN ME AND MY SINS!**
>
> Happy the man whose wrongs are forgiven, whose sin is taken away.
>
> I said, "I will go to Yahweh and confess my wrongs. You have forgiven me and my sins."
>
> Bless Yahweh, my soul! Remember his kindness in forgiving all your wrongs.

GOSPEL: Mt 6:14-15

> Yes, if you forgive others their failings, your heavenly Father will forgive you yours; but if you do not forgive others, your Father will not forgive your failings, either.

PETITIONS:

Response: **LORD, TEACH US HOW TO FORGIVE!**

For the times we hurt our brothers, sisters, moms and dads, we pray to the Lord. . . .

For the times we hurt our friends, we pray to the Lord. . . .

For the times when other people hurt us, we pray to the Lord. . . .

PREPARATION OF GIFTS:

Cross
Picture of family
Picture of friends
Bread, water and wine

Preparing ourselves:

We take up a cross to show that God forgives us for the times we say "No" to him.

We take up a picture of a family. Jesus wants us to say we are sorry when we hurt someone in our family and to forgive when someone hurts us.

We also take up a picture of our friends. Sometimes we fight with our friends. We can be like Jesus and say we are sorry and forgive when we get into quarrels.

We now take up the bread, water and wine. They will be changed into Jesus, the one who teaches us how to forgive.

SUGGESTED MUSIC:

"This Is My Commandment," **Hi, God! 2.**
"Our God Is a God of Love," **Hi, God! 2.**
"Jesus, You Have the Power to Heal," **Hi, God! 2.**
"What Shall I Do?" **Hi, God! 2.**
"Song of the Loving Father," **Hi, God! 2.**
"Making Peace," **Celebrating the Eucharist in Song.**

BANNER IDEA:

THEME:

> Jesus tells us, "Treat others as you would want them to treat you." We should not only love our families and friends, but also our enemies by doing kind things for them, playing with them, saying kind things, and praying for them.

READING: Lev 19:17-18 (paraphrased)

> I am God. You must not hate your brother in your heart. You must tell your neighbor openly of his offense. You must not bear a grudge. You must love your neighbor as yourself. I am God.

RESPONSORIAL PSALM: Prov 25:21; 24:17; 20:22 (paraphrased)

> Refrain: **LOVE YOUR ENEMIES. DO GOOD TO THEM!**

> If your enemy is hungry, give him something to eat; if thirsty, something to drink.

> Should your enemy fall, do not be happy. When he stumbles, do not be glad.

> Do not say, "I will get even." Put your hope in God and he will keep you safe.

GOSPEL: Lk 6:27-31, 35 (paraphrased)

> Listen to what I say to you: Love your enemies; do good to those who hate you; bless those who hurt you; pray for those who are bad to you. To the man who slaps you on one cheek, present the other cheek, too. Give to everyone who asks you. Treat others as you would like them to treat you. Love your enemies and do good and lend without receiving anything in return. Then you will have a great reward.

PETITIONS:

Response: **LORD, HELP US TO LOVE OUR ENEMIES!**

For the times we did not love our enemies, we pray to the Lord. . . .

For the times we were unkind and said unkind things, we pray to the Lord. . . .

For the people who find it hard to love, we pray to the Lord. . . .

PREPARATION OF GIFTS:

Picture of Jesus
Unhappy face
Smiley face
Bread, water and wine

Preparing ourselves:

We take up a picture of Jesus. Jesus is the one who shows us how to love.

We take up an unhappy face. This is how it feels when we don't love our enemies. We are sad . . . and so is the other person.

We also take up a smiley face. When we love our enemies, this is how we look! The person isn't an enemy anymore, he's now a friend!

We now bring up the bread, water and wine.

SUGGESTED MUSIC:

"This Is My Commandment," **Hi, God! 2.**
"What Shall I Do?" **Hi, God! 2.**
"Love That Is Kept Inside," **Hi God!**
"Reach Out," **Hi, God!**
"I Like God's Love," **Hi, God!**

BANNER IDEA:

GIFT IDEA:

Sad or unhappy face. . . .
    the way it feels when we do not love our enemies

Happy face . . .
    the way we feel when we love our enemies. They are no longer
enemies, but they are now friends!

THEME:

> We have learned many things about Jesus. Now we can go out and spread the good news! We can spread it to everyone we meet! We can tell people about Jesus by the things we say and the things we do. Sharing, forgiving, peacemaking, loving, being kind are some ways to tell people about Jesus.

Reading: Jer 1:4-8 (paraphrased)

> Yahweh said to me: "Before I formed you, I knew you. I have made you holy. I have made you a prophet to the nations." I said, "Ah, Yahweh, look, I do not know how to speak; I am a child!" But God said, "Do not say 'I am a child.' Go now to those to whom I send you and say what I tell you. Do not be afraid. I will protect you. It is God who speaks."

RESPONSORIAL PSALM: Is 43:10; 61:1 (paraphrased)

> Refrain: **HE HAS SENT ME TO BRING GOOD NEWS TO THE POOR!**
>
> You yourselves are my witnesses—it is God who speaks—my servants whom I have chosen.
>
> The spirit of the Lord has been given to me. God has made me holy.
>
> He has sent me to bring good news to the poor. He has sent me to make broken hearts happy again.

GOSPEL: Lk 9:1-6 (paraphrased)

Jesus called the Twelve together and gave them the power to cast out devils and to cure diseases. He sent them to proclaim the Kingdom of God and to heal. He said to them, "Take nothing for the journey; neither staff nor haversack, nor bread, nor money; and let none of you take a spare tunic. Whatever house you enter, stay there; and when you leave, let it be from there. As for those who do not welcome you, when you leave their town, shake the dust from your feet as a sign to them." So they set out and went from village to village proclaiming the Good News and healing everywhere.

PETITIONS:

Response: **LORD, HELP US TO SPREAD THE GOOD NEWS!**

That people will want to be your apostles and help spread the Good News, we pray to the Lord. . . .

For all people, so they may come to know and love Jesus as we do, we pray to the Lord. . . .

That people will come to know Jesus by the way we act and the things we say, we pray to the Lord. . . .

PREPARATION OF GIFTS:

Newspaper
Bible
Free-standing signs—WORDS, ACTIONS
Bread, water and wine

Preparing ourselves:

We bring up a newspaper to show this is where you find and read the news of the world today.

We take up a bible. We use the bible to learn more about Jesus so we can teach people and spread the Good News.

We also take up the signs WORDS and ACTIONS. We tell people about Jesus by the things we say and the things we do.

We offer our love with the bread, water and wine.

SUGGESTED MUSIC:

"Happiness," **Songs to Celebrate Life.**
"I've Heard His Word," **Songs to Celebrate Life.**
"Let's Go Forth," **Celebrating the Eucharist in Song.**
"Great Things Happen!" **Hi, God!**
"Yes, Lord, Yes," **Hi, God! 2.**

GIFT IDEA:

Draw the words ACTIONS and WORDS on two sheets of white paper each. Make sure the letters overlap one another so the words will stand freely. Cut out the words and glue them to cardboard. Display them on the altar or attach them to yarn and hang them from the altar.

BANNER IDEA:

FEBRUARY

FOLLOWING JESUS

THEME:

>Jesus is our leader! We follow him! Jesus shows us how to love, how to share, and how to be kind. The more we follow Jesus, the more we become like him! Let's be good followers today by showing a kindness to someone.

READING: 1 Jn 3:18-19 (paraphrased)

>My children, our love is not to be just words or talk, but something real. We must show our love by the things we do. This is the way we can tell the children of the truth—the followers of Jesus.

RESPONSORIAL PSALM: Prov 4:20-21,27; 11:25 (paraphrased)

>Refrain: **FOLLOW JESUS AND DO GOOD!**
>
>Listen carefully to the words I say. Do not let them out of your sight; keep them dear to your heart.
>
>Turn neither to the right nor to the left. Do good and keep away from bad things.
>
>Be generous and you will be happy. Help others and they will help you.

GOSPEL: Mt 9:9

>As Jesus was walking on from there he saw a man named Matthew sitting by the customs house and he said to him, "Follow me," and he got up and followed him.

PETITIONS:

Response: **HELP US TO BE GOOD FOLLOWERS!**

That all of us here always try to say "Yes" to God, we pray to the Lord. . . .

That we remember to pray for the people who do not follow Jesus, we pray to the Lord. . . .

That we try to help the people who need friends and are lonely, we pray to the Lord. . . .

PREPARATION OF GIFTS:

Footprints (made from construction paper)

Wrapped present (with notes inside showing ways we can be good followers)

Bread, water and wine

Preparing ourselves:

We take up some footprints to show that we use our feet to follow someone.

We also take up a present for Jesus. Inside are cards to Jesus showing the ways we can be good followers.

We offer our love with the bread, water and wine.

SUGGESTED MUSIC:

"I'm Following the Leader," **Songs to Celebrate Life.**

"Yes, Lord, Yes," **Hi, God! 2.**

"What God Is Like," **Hi, God! 2.**

"This Is My Commandment," **Hi, God! 2.**

"Happiness," **Songs to Celebrate Life.**

BANNER IDEA:

Make footprints from construction paper and glue then on the banner
or simply draw them on and color them with crayon.

PUT FOOTPRINTS IN THE AISLE TO THE ALTAR!!

Make 10 or more footprints from construction paper. Label each footprint with a different way that we can follow Jesus. During the homily, the priest can pick up the footprints and briefly discuss each one. Some ideas for the footprints are listed below.

Using our talents
Being kind
Forgiving others
Sharing
Praying to God
Helping our moms and dads
Helping others

THEME:

> Most of the Apostles were fishermen. We can be like fishermen, too! Instead of catching fish, Jesus wants us to spread the Good News to people. Let's start to spread the News of Jesus to everyone we meet today!

READING: II Pt 1:3-10 (paraphrased)

> God has given us all the things we need for life. He has also given us the promise of something very great and wonderful to come. Brothers, you have been called and chosen! Work all the harder!

RESPONSORIAL PSALM: Is 43:10, 13; 43:8 (paraphrased)

> Refrain: **I HAVE CHOSEN YOU SO THAT MEN CAN KNOW ME AND BELIEVE ME.**
>
> You yourselves are my witnesses. I am God who speaks. I have chosen you so that men can know me and believe me.
>
> You are my witnesses. I am God who speaks. I am God forever and ever.
>
> You are my witnesses. Is there any other God but me? There is no rock; I know of none.

GOSPEL: Mk 1:16-18

> As he was walking along by the Sea of Galilee, he saw Simon and his brother, Andrew, casting a net in the lake—for they were fishermen. And Jesus said to them, "Follow me and I will make you fishers of men." And at once they left their nets and followed him.

PETITIONS:

Response: **HELP US TO BE GOOD FISHERMEN!**

Jesus, help us to live like you did and spread your Good News and Love. We pray to the Lord. . . .

Help us always to say "Yes" to you and to show our families and friends your love. We pray to the Lord. . . .

Help us always to think of you . . . in people, in the animals, and in the beautiful world you have given us. We pray to the Lord. . . .

PREPARATION OF GIFTS:

Fishing pole
Construction-paper fish hung on a string (a "catch")
Bible
Bread, water and wine

Preparing ourselves:

We take up a fishing pole to show that the Apostles were fishermen.

We also take up a "catch" of fish. Jesus wants us to be fishers of men.

We now take up a bible. To spread the Good News, we need to learn about Jesus. We can learn many things in the bible.

We now offer our love as we take up the bread, water and wine.

SUGGESTED MUSIC:

"This Is My Commandment," **Hi, God! 2.**
"It's Up To Us," **Come Out.**
"Yes, Lord, Yes," **Hi, God! 2.**
"Great Things Happen," **Hi, God!**
"Reach Out," **Hi, God!**
"Love That Is Kept Inside," **Hi, God!**

GIFT IDEA:

> Make a "catch of fish" from brightly colored construction paper. Punch a hole in each fish. Hang fish from yarn using paper clips or by tying the yarn around the hole in each fish.   (see picture on next page)

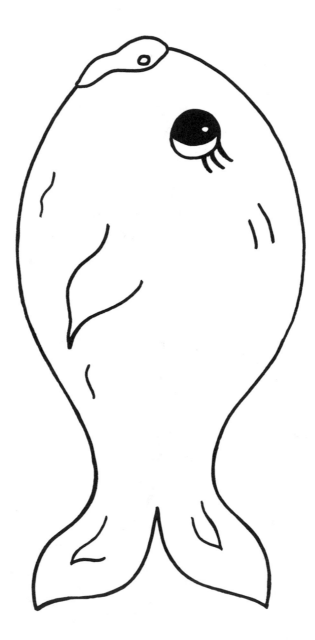

STRING OF FISH FOR GIFT

Decorate the lectern! Drape a fishnet around the stand and put some fish in the net. On the fish are homily hints for the priest saying the Mass. Different colors of fishnet are available at party stores for reasonable prices.

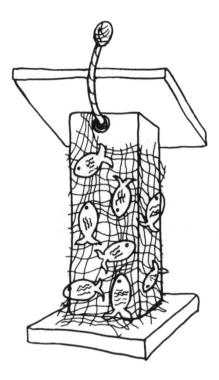

Also decorate the altar! Hang fish from a fishnet on the altar. Have each child make a fish with his name on it. We are fishers of men!!

Theme: (Built around the book, **The Giving Tree** by Shel Silverstein)

> **Our Mass today is about giving. Jesus wants us to give of ourselves. He wants us to be like the Giving Tree, and then we will be happy. The tree was always happy when she gave and shared part of herself. Let's be real givers like the Giving Tree today.**

READING: Sir 18:16-18 (paraphrased)

> **My sons, a word is better than a gift. And surely a word is better than a good present. But a good man is ready to give both a good word and a good gift.**

RESPONSORIAL PSALM: Prov 11:25; 15:4; 19:6 (paraphrased)

> Refrain: **GIVE AND YOU WILL BE HAPPY!**
>
> **Be giving and generous and you will be happy.**
>
> **Give kind words and you will be like a tree of life.**
>
> **The generous man is well-liked. He gives and the people become his friends.**

GOSPEL: Mk 9:41

> **If anyone gives you a cup of water to drink just because you belong to Jesus Christ, then I tell you solemnly, he will most certainly not lose his reward.**

PETITIONS:

Response: **HELP US TO BE GIVERS LIKE JESUS!**

That all of us here will become like the "Giving Tree," we pray to the Lord. . . .

That we give of ourselves by sharing, helping others, and using words to show our love, we pray to the Lord. . . .

That we pray for people who do not want to be like the "Giving Tree," we pray to the Lord. . . .

PREPARATION OF GIFTS:

Wrapped present
Collage containing "good words" (compliments)
Gift for Jesus (containing papers showing how we can become more like Jesus, more like the Giving Tree)
Bread, water and wine

Preparing ourselves:

For our gifts we take up a present. Giving a gift is one way to be like the "Giving Tree." Other ways are sharing and helping others.

We also take up a poster filled with words. Saying kind words and compliments is another way we can become like the "Giving Tree."

We now give a gift to Jesus. Inside are drawings and stories telling how we can become more giving like him.

We now take up the bread, water and wine.

SUGGESTED MUSIC:

It's Up To Us," **Come Out.**
"She's Just an Old Stump," **Come Out.**
"Reach Out," **Hi, God!**

GIFT IDEA:

Make a "Giving Tree" from cardboard and construction paper. You can even use a real branch instead of the cardboard trunk! On some of the leaves list ways in which we can give and be more like Jesus. When finished, stand by the lectern. The priest saying the Mass can pick and discuss some of the leaves during the homily.

PATTERN FOR LEAVES ON "BIG"
GIVING TREE

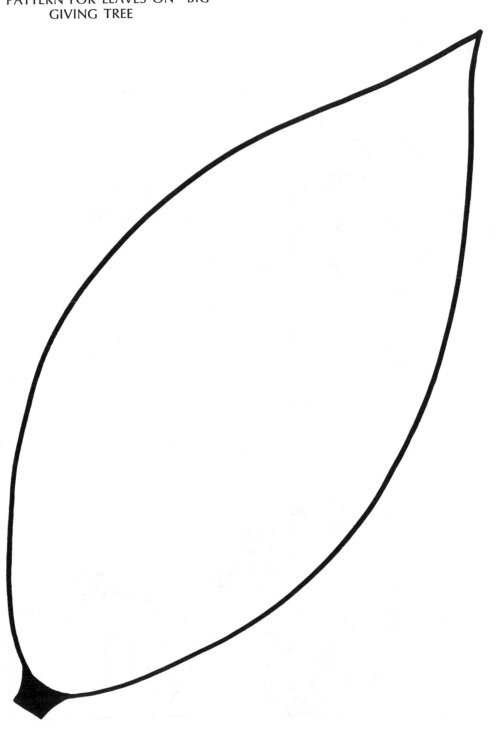

BANNER IDEA:

Make your banner into a big Giving Tree! Make your giving tree an apple tree, a pear tree, an orange tree, etc. Decorate the fruit with each of the children's names. We are all trying to be like the Giving Tree!

THEME:

> Today is the feast of St. Valentine. It is a day when we do something special for the people we love. God is love! He shows us how to love! Let's celebrate St. Valentine's Day in a special way today!

READING: I John 4:7-8, 11, 16 (paraphrased)

> My dear people, let us love one another, since love comes from God and everyone who loves is begotten by God and knows God. Anyone who fails to love can never have known God, because God is love. Since God has loved us so much, we too should love one another. God is love and anyone who lives in love lives in God and God lives in him.

RESPONSORIAL PSALM: Ps 11:5; 103:13,17 (paraphrased)

> Refrain: **GOD IS GOOD! HIS LOVE IS EVERLASTING!**
>
> Yes, God is good! His love is everlasting. He is faithful from age to age.
>
> As tenderly as a Father treats his children, so God loves his people.
>
> God's love for his people lasts from all eternity and is forever.

GOSPEL: Jn 15:9-11

> As the Father has loved me, so I have loved you. Remain in my love. If you keep my commandments, you will remain in my love, just as I have kept my Father's commandments, and remain in his love. I have told you this so that my joy may be in you and your joy may be complete.

PETITIONS:

> Response: **LORD, SHOW US HOW TO LOVE!**
>
> **For all our families on this special day, we pray to the Lord. . . .**
>
> **For our friends and brothers and sisters around the world, we pray to the Lord. . . .**
>
> **For the sick, lonely and unhappy people in the world, we pray to the Lord. . . .**

PREPARATION OF GIFTS:

> Big valentine
> Small valentines (ones the children will be passing around that day)
> Bread, water and wine
>
> Preparing ourselves:
>
> **We first take up a big valentine for God. We love God very much and he has shown us that he loves us very much, too.**
>
> **We also offer up the valentines which we will be passing out today.**
>
> **With the bread, water and wine, we give our love to God who also loves us.**

SUGGESTED MUSIC:

> "Hello Song," **Come Out.**
> "Let Us Go Up," **Songs to Celebrate Life.**
> "Our God Is a God of Love," **Hi, God! 2.**
> "This Is the Day," **Hi, God! 2.**
> "New Hope," **Hi, God! 2.**

BANNER IDEA:

MARCH

LENT

THEME:

Sometimes it's hard to say "Yes" to God. We feel like saying "No." That's what we call a temptation. It's not always easy. Even Jesus was tempted. But God tells us he will make us strong and make everything right again.

READING: I Pt 5:8-10 (paraphrased)

Be calm, but watchful, because your enemy, the devil, is prowling around like a roaring lion, looking for someone to eat. Stand up to him, strong in faith, knowing your brothers around the world are also suffering the same things. You will suffer only a little while. God will see that everything is all right again. He will give you strength. He will support you.

RESPONSORIAL PSALM: Pss 26:1-3; 25:4-5, 8-9 (paraphrased)

Refrain: **TEACH ME YOUR PATHS, O LORD!**

God is my judge! I always trust in God. Test me and put me to the trials; I will be loyal.

Teach me your paths, God. Set me in the way of truth. You are my God.

God is so good he teaches the way to sinners. He instructs the poor in the way.

GOSPEL: Mt 4:1-11 (paraphrased)

Then Jesus was led by the Spirit out into the wilderness to be tempted by the devil. He fasted for 40 days and 40 nights, after which he was very hungry and the tempter came and said to him, "If you are the Son of God, turn these stones into loaves of bread." But he replied,

"Scripture says, man does not live on bread alone, but on every word that comes from the mouth of God." The devil then took him to the holy city and said, "If you are the Son of God, throw yourself down, for scripture says: He will put you in his angels' charge, and they will support you on their hands in case you hurt your foot against a stone." Jesus said to him, "But scripture also says, you must not put the Lord your God to the test." Next, the devil took him to a very high mountain. The devil showed him all the kingdoms of the world. "I will give you all these, if you fall at my feet and worship me." Then Jesus said "Be off, Satan! For scripture says, you must worship the Lord your God and serve him alone." Then the devil left him, and the angels appeared and looked after him.

PETITIONS:

Response: **LORD, HELP US TO SAY YES!**

When we are weak and feel like saying "No" to you, we pray to the Lord. . . .

For all people, so we can learn to be strong, we pray to the Lord. . . .

For the people in the world who say "No" to you, we pray to the Lord. . . .

PREPARATION OF GIFTS:

Stones or rocks
"No" sign
Bread, water and wine

Preparing ourselves:

For our offertory gifts, we take up some stones to remind us that the devil even tempted Jesus.

We also take up a "No" sign. This will be our answer when the devil tries to tempt us.

We take up a bible. In the bible we learn more about Jesus. He teaches us how to live and how to be strong when we are tempted.

With the bread, water and wine we give ourselves to God, who strengthens us to do what is good.

SUGGESTED MUSIC:

"Father, We Adore You," **Hi, God! 2.**
"Friends, Friends, Friends," **Hi, God! 2.**
"This Is My Commandment," **Hi, God! 2.**
"I Want To Walk in the Presence of God," **Hi, God!**
"Yes, Lord, Yes," **Hi, God! 2.**

GIFT IDEAS:

Take up to the altar some big stones or rocks. Jesus was once tempted by the devil, too! He shows us how to be strong and to say "No" to the devil.

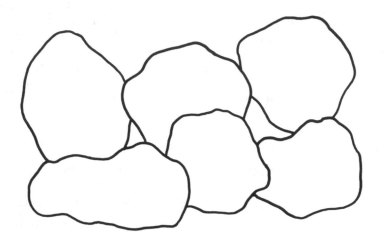

Also carry up a big "No" sign. Have the children make all different shapes and sizes of the word "No." This should be our answer when we are tempted.

BANNER IDEA:

    Children draw pictures of themselves or other people on the poster.

THEME:

Before Jesus died, he suffered very much. The people called him names; they put a crown of thorns on his head, and crucified him. We sometimes have little sufferings—little hurts. We can hurt on the outside or we can hurt on the inside. When we hurt on the outside, we can take medicines, use bandaids, or go to the doctor. But when we hurt on the inside, Jesus is the one who makes us better again. He will make us feel good inside.

READING: Rom 5:2-5 (paraphrased)

We have entered this state of grace that we can boast about looking forward to God's glory. But that isn't all we can boast about; we can boast about our sufferings. These sufferings make us patient and hopeful. This is a true hope. The love of God is in our hearts.

RESPONSE: Pss 107:13,14; 119:50 (paraphrased)

Refrain: **YOU HELP US WHEN WE SUFFER!**

They called to God in their trouble and he rescued them from their sufferings.

He released them from sadness and darkness and broke their chains. You have been my comfort in my suffering. Your promise gives me life.

GOSPEL: Mt 20:17-19 (paraphrased)

Jesus was going to Jerusalem, and on the way he took one of his Apostles and said to him, "Now we are going up to Jerusalem and the Son of Man is about to be given over to the chief priests and scribes. They will condemn him to death. They will hand him over to the pagans to be mocked and scourged and crucified and on the third day he will rise again."

110

PETITIONS:

Response: **LORD, HEAR OUR PRAYER!**

That all the sick people who are suffering will be well again soon, we pray to the Lord. . . .

For all the lonely people in the world, we pray to the Lord. . . .

That you fill us with your love and hope when we have little hurts, we pray to the Lord. . . .

PREPARATION OF GIFTS:

Band-Aids
cough medicine
bottles of medication
First-aid kit
tubes of medication
Picture of Jesus
Bread, water and wine

Preparing ourselves:

We first bring up some Band-Aids and medicines as our offertory gifts to God. These things make us well again when we have little hurts on the outside.

We also bring up a picture of Jesus. Jesus is the only one who makes us well again when we have little hurts on the inside.

We now take up the bread, water and wine and offer these to God.

SUGGESTED MUSIC:

"You Are My Brother," Part II, verses 3 and 4, **Hi, God! 2.**
Any Lenten songs

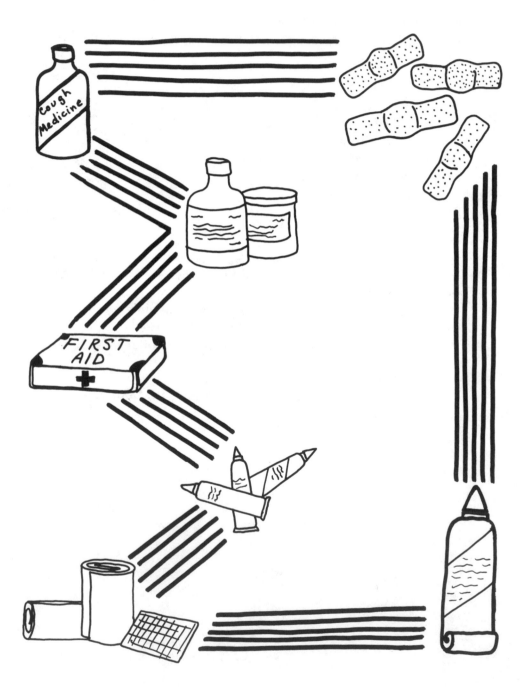

BANNER IDEA:

Children draw pictures below of things that make them feel better on the outside. The cross stands for Jesus—he makes the inside better.

THEME:

> Today is St. Patrick's Day! And most of us have green on to celebrate! St. Patrick was a very special man who always tried to say "Yes" to God. He was a good follower and taught the people about God. He also used a shamrock to tell the people about God.

READING: Is 6:8-10 (paraphrased)

> I heard the voice of the Lord saying: "Whom will I send? Who will be my messenger?" I answered, "Here I am. Send me!" God said, "Go and talk to these people so they will understand with their heart and learn to live the way they should."

RESPONSORIAL PSALM: Ps 117:1-2 (paraphrased)

> Refrain: **GO AND TELL THE GOOD NEWS!**
>
> Praise the Lord, all you people!
>
> Praise the Lord for his love is strong.
>
> Praise the Lord because he loves us forever.

GOSPEL: Mt 16:24 (paraphrased)

> Then Jesus said to his disciples, "If anyone wants to be a follower of mine, let him forget about himself, take up his cross and follow me."

PETITIONS:

Response: **LORD, HELP US TO BE GOOD FOLLOWERS!**

For all of us here, so we can act more like Jesus every day, we pray to the Lord. . . .

For people everywhere, so they can say "Yes" to you, like St. Patrick did, we pray to the Lord. . . .

For the people who say "No" to you, we pray to the Lord. . . .

PREPARATION OF GIFTS:

Shamrock
Book of Jesus
Bread, water and wine

Preparing ourselves:

For our Offertory gifts, we first bring up a shamrock. St. Patrick used this to tell the people about God the Father, Jesus and the Spirit.

We also take up our book of Jesus which we have made. The pages show ways we can follow Jesus and be more like him.

We now offer our love with the bread, water and wine.

SUGGESTED MUSIC:

"Yes, Lord, Yes," **Hi, God! 2.**
"Father, We Adore You," **Hi, God! 2.**
"Let's Go Forth," **Celebrating the Eucharist in Song**
"Happiness," **Songs to Celebrate Life**
"I've Heard His Word" **Songs to Celebrate Life**

OFFERTORY GIFT:

Make an accordion-pleat booklet from construction paper and cardboard. On each of the pages, write some of the things Jesus teaches us about. Have the children decorate the pages with their drawings.

Take up the booklet about Jesus at the offertory procession and display it on or in front of the altar.

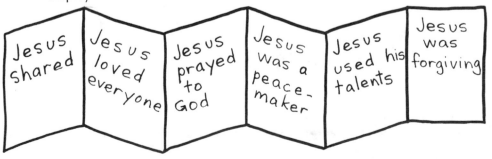

BANNER IDEA:

THEME:

> Today is really special! It is the first day of spring! New flowers, new plants and new trees are beginning to grow! The animals are beginning to come out, too! God made all these beautiful things for us to enjoy. He makes them new for us every year. Let's enjoy all these wonderful things today that God has made!

READING: Is 42:5 (paraphrased)

> God created the heavens and spread them out. He gave shape to the earth and what comes from it. He gave breath to its people and life to the creatures that move in it.

RESPONSORIAL PSALM: Ps 104:14,19,30 (paraphrased)

> Refrain: **THE EARTH IS FULL OF THINGS YOU HAVE MADE!**
>
> **The earth has all it needs. Fresh grass grows for cattle and plants grow for men to use.**
>
> **You made the moon to tell the seasons. The sun knows when to set.**
>
> **You give breath and fresh life begins. You keep renewing the world.**

GOSPEL: Jn 1:3 (paraphrased)

> God made all things. Not one thing has its being but through him.

PETITIONS:

> Response: **LORD, HELP US TO TREAT YOUR WORLD WITH KINDNESS!**
>
> So we can show our love to all our brothers and sisters in the world, we pray to the Lord. . . .
>
> So we can be kind and good to the animals you have given us to enjoy, we pray to the Lord. . . .

117

So we use the trees, plants, and other things in your world carefully, we pray to the Lord. . . .

PREPARATION OF GIFTS:

Flowers
Small shrub
Stuffed animal
Collage of people
Bread, water and wine

Preparing ourselves:

For our Offertory gifts, we first take up some flowers and a small shrub. These are signs that spring is coming. New things are beginning to grow.

We also take up a stuffed animal to show that now the animals are starting to come out and the birds are coming home.

We also take up a collage of people. We are part of God's creation, too. God wants us to treat each other with love.

We now take up the bread, water and wine.

SUGGESTED MUSIC:

"All Your Gifts of Life," **Hi, God! 2.**
"Hello Song," **Come Out.**
"Come Out," **Come Out.**
"Make a Joyful Noise," **Songs to Celebrate Life.**
"Thank You, Lord," **Songs to Celebrate Life.**
"Special Places," **Songs to Celebrate Life.**
"Celebrate Life," **Songs to Celebrate Life.**
"Giving Thanks For Creation," **Celebrating the Eucharist in Song.**

BANNER IDEA:

Have the children draw big flowers for the banner. Write the signs of spring inside.

APRIL
LENT
CONTINUED

COMING HOME

THEME:

The prodigal son left home and went away. But after he wasted all his money, he was sorry about the things he had done. He came home. Sometimes we wander away—we say "No" to God. But we come home again, too! We come back to God. God welcomes us home! He forgives us for straying. He's happy we're home again!

READING: Is 1:16-19 (paraphrased)

"Stop doing bad things. Learn to do good and help the poor. Come, let us talk this over," says God. "Though your sins are like scarlet, they shall be as white as snow, though they are red as crimson, they shall be like wool. If you are willing to obey, you shall eat the good things of the earth."

RESPONSORIAL PSALM: Ps 85:4,6,7 (paraphrased)

Refrain: **BRING US BACK, LORD!**

Bring us back, God our savior. Do not be angry with us.

Give us life again, so we can rejoice and be happy in you.

Yahweh, show us your love. Grant us your saving help.

GOSPEL: LK 15:11-32 (paraphrased)

A man had two sons. The younger said to his father, "Father, let me have the share of the estate that would come to me." So the father divided the property between them. The younger son packed his things and left for a distant country, where he wasted all his money. Now that he had no money, he got a job on a farm feeding the pigs. No one would give him any food to eat, so he ate the food the pigs were eating. After a while he thought, My father's servants have more food than they want, and here I am starving to death! I will leave this place and go home. I will say to my father, "Father, I have sinned against heaven and against you. I no longer deserve to be called your son; treat me as one of your servants." So he left and went home. His father saw him coming. He ran to the boy and hugged and kissed him. The son said, "Father, I have sinned against heaven and you. I no longer deserve to be called your son." But the father told his servants to bring the best robe for his son and to kill the fattest calf so they could celebrate with a meal. "This son of mine was dead and now has come back to life; he was lost and now he is found!" And they began to celebrate. When the older son found out what was happening, he was very angry. He told his father, "All these years I have slaved for you and never disobeyed. You never offered a fattened calf for me to celebrate with my friends. But you do it for this son who wasted all his money." The father said, "My son, you are always with me, and all I have is yours. But we should rejoice now because your brother was dead and has come to life. He was lost and now he is found."

PETITIONS:

Response: **BRING US HOME TO YOU, JESUS!**

For all of us here when we wander away from God, we pray to the Lord. . . .

For people who find it hard to say "Yes" to you, we pray to the Lord. . . .

For the people who do not show their love for you by loving and forgiving others, we pray to the Lord. . . .

PREPARATION OF GIFTS:

Suitcase
Clay or papier-mache model of your church
Bread, water and wine

Preparing ourselves:

For our gifts to God, we first take up a suitcase. This reminds us of the times when we wander away from God and say "No" to him, like the prodigal son who went away.

We also take up a model of our church to show that we come back home to God. God welcomes us and is happy we are back home with him!

We now bring up the bread, water and wine which will be changed into Jesus.

SUGGESTED MUSIC:

"Song of the Loving Father," **Hi, God! 2.**
"Jesus, Jesus," **Hi, God! 2.**
"Peace Is Flowing Like a River," **Hi, God! 2.**

BANNER IDEA:

When we go away, we take suitcases. We also bring them with us when we come home! Have the children draw suitcases on your banner.

THEME:

> The night before Jesus died, he gave us a new commandment. It was to love one another. We show our love for Jesus by loving others. Let's show and share our love today with the people we meet. Then we will be good followers of Jesus.

READING: Rom 13:8-10 (paraphrased)

> If you love your fellow man you have done what you should. All the commandments can be put into this one command: You must love your neighbor as yourself. Love is the one thing that cannot hurt your neighbor; that is why it is the answer to every one of the commandments.

RESPONSORIAL PSALM: Pss 85:7,12; 86:12-13 (paraphrased)

> Refrain: **SHOW US YOUR LOVE!**
>
> Your people rejoice in you. Yahweh, show us your love.
>
> God himself gives us happiness as the soil gives us a harvest.
>
> I glorify your name forever. Your love for me has been so great.

GOSPEL: Jn 13:33-35

> My little children, I shall not be with you much longer. You will look for me, and as I told the Jews, where I am going, you cannot come. I give you a new commandment: Love one another. By this love you have for one another everyone will know that you are my disciples.

PETITIONS:

Response: **HELP US TO LOVE OTHERS!**

For the sick people in the world who need to be helped, we pray to the Lord. . . .

For the unhappy people who have no friends, we pray to the Lord. . . .

For our families and friends, we pray to the Lord. . . .

PREPARATION OF GIFTS:

Dish towel and broom
Blackboard eraser and crayons
"Get Well" card
Bread, water and wine

Preparing ourselves:

We first bring up a dish towel and a broom to remind us that we can show our love at home for our families by helping them.

We also take up a blackboard eraser and some crayons to show that we can show our love for others at school by helping and by sharing.

We now bring up a "Get Well" card. This reminds us to show our love for the people who are sick.

We now bring up the bread, water and wine which will be changed into Jesus, our brother who loves us and wants us to love others.

SUGGESTED MUSIC:

"Love That Is Kept Inside," **Hi, God!**
"What Makes Love Grow?" **Hi, God!**
"Reach Out," **Hi, God!**
"This Is My Commandment," **Hi, God! 2.**

BANNER IDEA:

> For something different, turn your banner into a big gameboard. The children think of things to put in the squares. After Mass, play the game!

THEME:

> The apostles loved Jesus very much. But one day Jesus told Peter he would deny him three times. Peter couldn't believe this! He loved Jesus and wouldn't hurt Jesus. But Peter did deny Jesus three times, just as Jesus had said. Sometimes, we might act like Peter. Who, me? Yes—maybe you! Let's ask Jesus to make us strong.

READING: Heb 10:35,37-38 (paraphrased)

> Be confident now and your reward will be great. Only a little while now and the one who is coming will come. The good man will live by faith. But if he draws back, I will not be happy with him.

RESPONSORIAL PSALM: Is 45:21,22; 46:9 (paraphrased)

> Refrain: **THERE IS NO OTHER GOD BESIDES ME!**
>
> Am I not Yahweh? There is no other God besides me. I am your savior.
>
> Turn to me and be saved, all the ends of the earth, for I am the only God.
>
> I am the only God. There is no God like me.

GOSPEL: Mt 26:31-35 (paraphrased)

> Jesus said to them, "You will all lose faith in me this night, for scripture says: I will strike the shepherd and the sheep of the flock will be scattered. But after my resurrection I will go before you to Galilee." At this Peter said, "Everyone might lose faith in you. But I never will." Jesus answered him, "I tell you, tonight before the cock crows, you will have disowned me three times." Peter said to him, "Even if I die with you, I will never disown you." And all the Apostles said the same.

PETITIONS:

Response: **LORD, MAKE US STRONG!**

For all the people who do not believe in you, Jesus, we pray to the Lord. . . .

For all the people who do not want to be more like you, we pray to the Lord. . . .

For all of us here when we start to act like Peter did that night, we pray to the Lord. . . .

PREPARATION OF GIFTS:

Big question mark
Weights
Picture of Jesus
Bread, water and wine

Preparing ourselves:

We first bring up a big question mark as an Offertory gift. Peter denied Jesus. He didn't think he would. We don't think we will, either. Who, me?

We also take up some weights. People use these to make themselves strong on the outside.

Now we bring up a picture of Jesus. He makes us strong on the inside.

We bring up the bread, water and wine. We believe in Jesus and love him.

SUGGESTED MUSIC:

"I'm Following the Leader," **Songs to Celebrate Life.**

"Yes, Lord, Yes," **Hi, God! 2.**

"Children of the Lord," **Hi, God! 2.**

"Happiness," **Songs to Celebrate Life.**

BANNER IDEA:

Have the children make many different sizes of question marks.

THEME:

Today is Easter . . . the day Jesus rose from the dead! He suffered for us and even died for us. But three days later he rose again! See how much Jesus loves us!

READING: I Cor 15:3-4 (paraphrased)

I taught you what I have been taught myself. That is, that Jesus died for our sins, just like the scriptures said and He was buried and He rose to life on the third day, just as the scriptures said.

RESPONSORIAL PSALM: Ps 117:1-2 (paraphrased)

Refrain: **ALLELUIA! ALLELUIA!**

Alleluia! Praise God, all you nations of people!

Alleluia! Praise God for his love is strong!

Alleluia! Praise God for he loves us forever!

GOSPEL: Jn 20:1-10 (paraphrased)

It was very early and dark when Mary of Magdala came to the tomb. She saw that the stone had been moved away from the tomb. She went running to Simon Peter and the other disciple, the one Jesus loved. She said, "They have taken the Lord out of the tomb and we don't know where they have laid him." Peter and the other disciple ran together to the tomb. But the other disciple ran faster and reached the tomb first. He bent down and saw the linen clothes lying on the ground, but did not go in. Simon Peter now came up and went right into the tomb. They saw and believed. Till this moment they had failed to understand the teaching of scripture, that he must rise from the dead. The disciples then went home again.

PETITIONS:

Response: **RISEN LORD, HEAR US!**

That all people in the world will have a happy Easter, we pray to the Lord. . . .

That we show our love for others just as Jesus has shown that he loves us, we pray to the Lord. . . .

That we will be filled with peace and love on this happy day, we pray to the Lord. . . .

PREPARATION OF GIFTS:

Cross
Lilies
Easter basket (full)
Bread, water and wine

Preparing ourselves:

For our Offertory gifts, we first bring up a cross to show that Jesus loved us so much that he suffered and died for us.

We also take up some lilies. Three days after Jesus died on the cross for us, he rose from the dead. That's the Good News of Easter!!

We now take up an Easter basket and hope that everyone here will have a very happy Easter Day!!

We bring up the bread, water and wine with our love.

SUGGESTED MUSIC:

"Are Not Our Hearts," **Hi, God!**
"Rejoice in the Lord Always," **Hi, God!**
"You Are My Brother," verse 4, **Hi, God! 2.**
"This Is the Day," **Hi, God! 2.**
"Oh Yes, Lord Jesus Lives," **Hi, God! 2.**
"New Hope," **Hi, God! 2.**

BANNER IDEA:

THEME:

After Jesus rose from the dead, he appeared to his Apostles. But one of them, Thomas, wouldn't believe this, until he really saw Jesus and touched his wounds. Thomas doubted Jesus. He didn't believe him. Let's be strong and always believe in Jesus and what he tells us.

READING: I John 5:5, 10-12 (paraphrased)

Who can overcome the world? Only the man who believes that Jesus is the Son of God. Everybody who believes in the Son of God has this testimony inside him: God has given us eternal life and this life is his Son. Anyone who has this Son has life, anyone who does not have the Son does not have life.

RESPONSORIAL PSALM: Ps 84:12; 31:6-7; 56:4 (paraphrased)

Refrain: **HAPPY THE MAN WHO PUTS HIS TRUST IN YOU!**

My God, happy the man who puts his trust in you!

I put my trust in God. I will be happy and rejoice in your love.

I put my trust in God and fear nothing. What can men do to me when I trust you?

GOSPEL: Jn 20:24-29 (paraphrased)

Thomas, called the Twin, who was one of the Apostles, was not with them when Jesus appeared. When the disciples told him that they had seen the Lord, he answered, "Unless I see the holes that the nails made in his hands and can put my finger into the holes they made, and unless I can put my hand into his side, I refuse to believe." Eight days later, Thomas and the rest of the Apostles were in the house again. The doors were closed, but Jesus came in and stood with them. "Peace be with you," he said. Then he said to Thomas, "Put your fingers here; look, here are my hands. Give me your hand; put it into my side. Doubt no longer, but believe." Thomas replied, "My Lord and my God!" Jesus said to him, "You believe because you can see me; happy the people who have not seen and yet believe."

PETITIONS:

Response: **LORD, HELP ALL PEOPLE BELIEVE IN YOU!**

For people who do not believe in Jesus, we pray to the Lord. . . .

For all of us here, when we act like Thomas did, we pray to the Lord. . . .

For all our special intentions, we pray to the Lord. . . .

PREPARATION OF GIFTS:

Construction-paper hands
"We Believe in You" sign
Bread, water and wine

Preparing ourselves:

We first take up some construction-paper hands to remind us that Thomas did not believe that Jesus rose from the dead.

We also take up our "We Believe in You" sign. This tells how we feel about Jesus.

We now take up the bread, water and wine. This will soon be Jesus, whom we love and trust.

SUGGESTED MUSIC:

"Jesus, Jesus," **Hi, God! 2.**
"Father, We Adore You," **Hi, God! 2.**
"You Are My Brother," part II **Hi, God! 2.**
"Oh Yes, Lord Jesus Lives," **Hi, God! 2.**
"I Believe in the Sun," **Hi, God!**
"Are Not Our Hearts," **Hi, God!**
"Rejoice in the Lord Always," **Hi, God!**

GIFT IDEAS:

Make a "We Believe in You" sign on posterboard and bring it up in the Offertory procession. It can be put on the altar or leaned up against the altar.

Make your sign from construction paper. Cut the letters out of brightly colored paper. Glue or staple them to yarn or string. Bring the sign up at the Offertory procession and have the children hang it from the altar for all to see!

BANNER IDEA:

Have the children trace their hands on the banner. Then have them write their names on their hands. All of us believe in Jesus!

THEME:

Jesus asked his apostle, Peter, "Do you really love me?" Peter answered, "Yes Lord, you know I love you." Then Jesus said, "Feed my sheep." Jesus was really telling Peter to take care of his people . . . to lead them and teach them. We are part of this people, part of the Church.

READING: Eph 2:19-22 (paraphrased)

You are part of God's household. You are part of a building that has Jesus himself for the cornerstone. All grow into one holy temple in the Lord. And you, too, are being built into a house where God lives, in the Spirit.

RESPONSORIAL PSALM: Ps 72:8, 11, 15 (paraphrased)

Refrain: **HIS EMPIRE WILL STRETCH FROM SEA TO SEA!**

His empire shall stretch from sea to sea; from the river to the end of the earth.

All kings will honor him. All nations will become his servants.

Prayer will be offered to him all the time. Blessings given to him all day long.

GOSPEL: John 21:15-17

After the meal Jesus said to Simon Peter, "Simon, son of John, do you love me more than these others do?" He answered, "Yes, Lord, you know I love you." Jesus said to him, "Feed my lambs." A second time he said to him, "Simon, son of John, do you love me?" He replied, "Yes, Lord, you know I love you." Jesus said to him, "Look after my sheep." Then he said to him a third time, "Simon, son of John, do you love me?" Peter was upset that he asked him the third time, "Do you love me?" and said, "Lord, you know everything; you know I love you." Jesus said to him, "Feed my sheep."

PETITIONS:

Response: **LORD, HEAR THE PRAYERS OF YOUR PEOPLE!**

So all people will come to know that they are part of God's Church and flock, we pray to the Lord. . . .

So we may be strong to be good followers of Jesus and good members of Christ's Church, we pray to the Lord. . . .

So we may be good listeners and do what you want us to do, we pray to the Lord. . . .

PREPARATION OF GIFTS:

Paper or cardboard sheep
One of Father's vestments
Bread, water and wine

Preparing ourselves:

We first bring up some sheep. The sheep have our names on them to show that we are part of the sheep . . . part of the flock . . . part of the church.

We also take up one of Father's vestments. He is one of the leaders of the church that Jesus founded, along with the bishops and the pope. These people lead us and teach us about Jesus.

We now bring up the bread, water and wine. These will be changed into Jesus, the one who started the church.

SUGGESTED MUSIC:

"Do You Really Love Me?" **Hi, God!**
"God Is Building a House," **Hi, God! 2.**
"We are the Body of Christ," **Hi, God! 2.**
"Come Along with Me to Jesus," **Hi, God! 2.**

GIFT IDEA:

Make several of the sheep below. Have the children write their names on the sheep. One class should be able to fit all their names on one of the sheep . . . each class will have its own sheep. Take all of them up at Offertory time and stand them in front of the altar.

BANNER IDEA:

Make a big lamb. Punch holes in the top and hang it from the lectern.

Smaller sheep could be made and, at the Sign of Peace, the children could hand their lambs to someone else and say, "Peace be with you! You are part of God's people, his Church!"

THEME:

> Do you know what a king is? Do you know what a king does? Today, let's think about kings and kingdoms. God is our king and we live in his kingdom! We are part of his kingdom! Since God is our king, he leads and teaches us. He teaches us about the way we should live!

READING: Dan 2:44-45 (paraphrased)

> In the time of these kings, the God of heaven will set up a kingdom which will never end and never be destroyed. This kingdom will be made of all the other kingdoms. And it will last forever.

RESPONSORIAL PSALM: Ps 47:6,7,9 (paraphrased)

> Refrain: **GOD, KING OF THE WHOLE WORLD!**
>
> Let the music sound for our God; let it sound! Let the music sound for our king; let it sound!
>
> God is king of the whole world. Play your best in his honor!
>
> Every place in the world belongs to God. He is the king.

GOSPEL: Mt 13:31-32 (paraphrased)

> Jesus told them another story: "The kingdom of heaven is like a mustard seed which a man took and planted in his field. It is the smallest of all the seeds, but when it is grown, it is the biggest shrub of all and becomes a tree so that the birds of the air come and make their home in its branches."

PETITIONS:

Response: **LORD, HEAR THE PRAYERS OF YOUR KINGDOM!**

For all of us in your kingdom who love you very much, we pray to the Lord. . . .

For the people in your kingdom who find it hard to say "Yes" to you, we pray to the Lord. . . .

For the sick and unhappy people in your kingdom, so they will be well and glad again, we pray to the Lord. . . .

PREPARATION OF GIFTS:

Construction-paper crown
Cardboard people
Child's drawing of Jesus
Bread, water and wine

Preparing ourselves:

We first take up a crown to show that God is our king who loves us very much.

We also take up some pictures of people. These show that all of us belong to God's kingdom.

We now bring up a picture of Jesus, who shows us what God is like and teaches us about God's love, and how we should live in God's kingdom.

We offer our love with the bread, water and wine.

SUGGESTED MUSIC:

"Show and Tell," **Songs to Celebrate Life.**
"We Are the Body of Christ," **Hi, God! 2.**
"God Is Building a House," **Hi, God! 2.**
"Reign, Lord," **Hi, God!**
"Oh, How I Love Jesus," **Hi, God!**

BANNER IDEA:

Make a crown like the one below. Have the children write their names inside. We are all part of God's kingdom! No words are needed on the banner. The crown tells it all!

THEME:

> This special day is Mother's Day. Mothers do so much for us! They cook for us, make us better when we are sick, make us feel good, and help us! They love us very much and we really love them! Thanks God, for giving us our moms!

READING: Dt 5:16 (paraphrased)

> Honor your father and your mother. Love them. This is what God wants you to do. If you do this, you will have long life and live in the land that God has given you.

RESPONSORIAL PSALM: Prov 6:20,21,22 (paraphrased)

> Refrain: **LISTEN TO YOUR MOTHER'S TEACHING!**

> Listen to your father's teaching. Listen to your mother's teaching, my son.

> Take their teachings in your heart and always use them.

> When you walk, they will help you; when you lie down, they will watch over you. When you wake, they will talk with you.

GOSPEL: Jn 19:25-27 (paraphrased)

> By the cross of Jesus stood his mother and his mother's sister. Seeing his mother and the disciple he loved standing next to her, Jesus said to his mother, "Woman, this is your son." He then said to the disciple, "This is your mother." From then on, the disciple made a place for her in his home.

PETITIONS:

Response: **LORD, BLESS MOTHERS EVERYWHERE!**

For our mothers who always help us, take care of us and love us, we pray to the Lord. . . .

For all mothers in the world, we pray to the Lord. . . .

So our mothers will always be happy and full of your love, we pray to the Lord. . . .

PREPARATION OF GIFTS:

Rolling pin and iron
Kleenex and Band-Aids
Big, big heart (made from construction paper)
Bread, water and wine

Preparing ourselves:

We first bring up a rolling pin and an iron to show that our mothers do many things for us.

We also bring up some Kleenex and Band-Aids. Our moms make us feel better when we are sick.

We take up a big heart to show that we love our moms very, very much. We now bring up the bread, water and wine.

SUGGESTED MUSIC:

"Thank You, Lord," **Songs to Celebrate Life.**
"People Who Care," **Songs to Celebrate Life.**
"Songs for Everyone," **Songs to Celebrate Life.**
"A Great Beginning," **Songs to Celebrate Life.**
"Hello Song," **Come Out.**
"Hail Mary," **Hi, God! 2.**

BANNER IDEA:

Have the children invite their moms to this celebration. At the sign of peace, have the children give their moms something they have made for them—a card, a picture, something from clay, a flower, etc.

(ATTACH PICTURES OF THE CHILDREN WITH THEIR MOMS, OR HAVE THE CHILDREN DRAW A PICTURE OF THEMSELVES WITH THEIR MOMS)

JUNE
———
END OF
THE YEAR

THEME:

> Today is the last day of school! We did many things together this year. We learned a lot of new things, played together and prayed together. Let's celebrate the last day of school by singing, praying, and listening now at Mass. See you again in the fall!

READING: II Cor 13:11-13 (paraphrased)

> In the meantime, brothers, we wish you happiness. Try to grow perfect; help one another. Be united and live in peace; then the God of love and peace will be with you. Greet one another with a holy kiss. May the love of God be with all of you.

RESPONSORIAL PSALM: Ps 112:1,9,2 (paraphrased)

> Refrain: **HAPPY THE PEOPLE WHO LOVE GOD!**
>
> Happy the man who loves God and keeps his commandments.
>
> Men who do this will always be honored.
>
> The children of these men will always be blessed.

GOSPEL: Jn 14:18-21 (paraphrased)

> I will not leave you orphans. I will come back to you. In a short time, the world will no longer see me. But you will see me, because I live and you will live. On that day you will understand that I am in my Father and you in me and I in you. Anybody who keeps my commandments will be loved by me and my Father.

PETITIONS:

Response: **LORD, BE WITH US THROUGH THE SUMMER!**

So we will be your good followers throughout the summer, we pray to the Lord. . . .

So we can show what we have learned about you to others, we pray to the Lord. . . .

So everyone has a happy and fun-filled summer, we pray to the Lord. . . .

PREPARATION OF GIFTS:

Beach ball
"Good-bye" sign
Bible
Bread, water and wine

Preparing ourselves:

For our Offertory gifts, we first bring up a beach ball. We hope that everyone has a happy summer and lots of fun!

We also bring up a "Good-bye" sign. We will see most of you in the summer and we will see all of you again in the fall.

We also bring up a bible to remind us that we are followers of Jesus. And that we will show this in the summer by the things we say and the things we do.

We now bring up the bread, water and wine which will be changed into Jesus.

SUGGESTED MUSIC:

"Let's Go Forth," **Celebrating the Eucharist in Song.**
"Make a Joyful Noise," **Songs to Celebrate Life.**
"Goodbye, Goodbye," **Songs to Celebrate Life.**
"His Banner Over Me," verses 4 & 5, **Hi, God!**

GIFT IDEA:

These letters are all mixed up! Put them together to make the word "Good-bye." Make them from construction paper with cardboard backing and take up at the Offertory to set in front of the altar. Each letter stands for something:

G—God. He loves us very much.

O—our. Our Father is God. We are all brothers and sisters.

O—others. That's whom Jesus wants us to love.

D—disciples. We can be disciples, followers of Jesus, too.

B—bible. We can learn more about Jesus from this book.

Y—year. This year we learned a lot more about Jesus.

E—everyone. Hope everyone has a happy summer!

GOOD-BYE!!!!!!

BANNER IDEA:

Make the word "Good-bye" on your banner. Also make some people holding up the sign.

THEME:

> Today is Father's Day. We really love our dads. They do so much for us. . . . They help us, teach us new things, take us places, and love us. Thank you, God, for our dads!

READING: Eph 6:1-3 (paraphrased)

> Children, obey your mother and your father. That is what you must do. The commandment has a promise with it: Honor and love your father and mother, and the promise is . . . and you will be happy and live a long life in the land.

RESPONSORIAL PSALM: Sir 3:1-2, 6, 14 (paraphrased)

> Refrain: **BE KIND TO YOUR FATHER. YOUR FATHER WILL NEVER FORGET IT!**
>
> Children, listen to me, your father. Do what I tell you and you will be safe.
>
> Long life comes to him who honors and loves his father.
>
> Be kind to your father. Your father will never forget it.

GOSPEL: Mt 21:28-31 (paraphrased)

> What do you think? A father had two sons. He went and said to the first, "My boy, go and work in the vineyards today." He answered, "I will not go," but afterwards thought better of it and went. The man then went and said the same thing to the second son who answered, "Certainly, sir," but did not go. Which of the two did what his father wanted him to?

PETITIONS:

Response: **LORD, BLESS FATHERS EVERYWHERE!**

For our fathers who help us, love us and teach us, we pray to the Lord. . . .

For fathers everywhere in the world, we pray to the Lord. . . .

That our dads will always be happy, we pray to the Lord. . . .

PREPARATION OF GIFTS:

Hammer and saw
Books
Bread, water and wine

Preparing ourselves:

We first bring up a hammer and a saw to show that our dads help us in lots of different ways.

We also bring up some books. Our dads teach us many things, too.

We now take up the bread, water and wine. We offer these to God, who is everybody's Father.

SUGGESTED MUSIC:

"Hello Song," **Come Out.**
"Thank You, Lord," **Songs to Celebrate Life.**
"Songs for Everyone," **Songs to Celebrate Life.**
"People Who Care," **Songs to Celebrate Life.**

BANNER IDEA:

Make a big, big tie with collar. Have the children decorate the tie with pictures of their dads.

Silverstein, Shel, **The Giving Tree,** New York: Harper & Row, 1964.

Steinmueller, John E. and Kathryn Sullivan, **Catholic Biblical Encyclopedia,** New York: Joseph F. Wagner, Inc., 1956.

The Jerusalem Bible (Reader's Edition), Garden City, New York: Doubleday and Company, Inc., 1968.

Music suggested in this book may be obtained at the following addresses:

Hi, God! (Album and Songbook), North American Liturgy Resources, 300 East McMillan Street, Cincinnati, Ohio 45219

Hi, God! 2 (Album and Songbook), North American Liturgy Resources, 2110 W. Peoria Avenue, Phoenix, Arizona 85029

Celebrating the Eucharist in Song (Songbook), Arena Lettres, 432 Park Avenue South, New York, New York 10016

Songs to Celebrate Life (Songbook), Raven Music Company, 4107 Woodland Park Avenue, N., Seattle, Washington 98103

Come Out (Album and Songbook), World Library Publications, Inc., 2145 Central Parkway, Cincinnati, Ohio 45214